Name _____

At the Toy Store

Count. Write the number.

A.

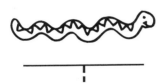

B.

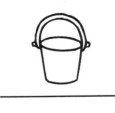

Write the numbers 1 through 6.

C. ___ ___ ___ ___ ___ ___

FS-32068 First Grade Math Review

Counting Zoo

Count. Write the number.

A.
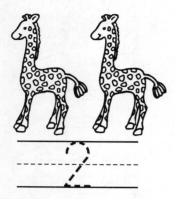

2

B.

C.

D.

E.

F.

Write the numbers 1 through 6.

G.

FS-32068 First Grade Math Review

Pegboard Match

Color.

A.

4 four

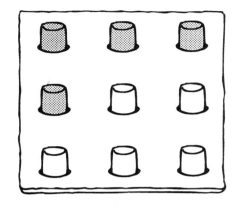

1 one

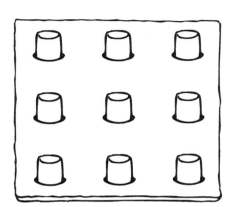

B.

5 five

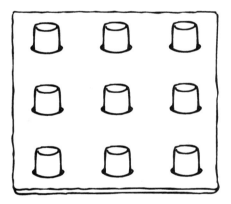

3 three

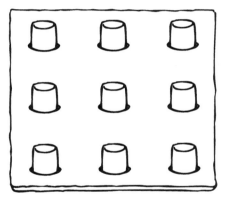

C.

2 two

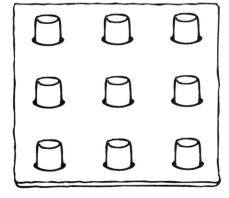

6 six

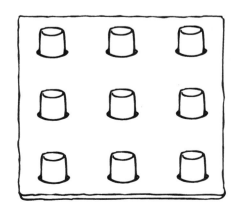

FS-32068 First Grade Math Review

Name_____

At the Circus

Color.

A. **2**
two

B. **1**
one

C. **4**
four

D. **5**
five

E. **6**
six

F. **3**
three

Name _____

Fishy Schools

Count. Write the number.

A.

_ _ _ _ _ _ _ _ _

B.

_ _ _ _ _ _ _ _ _

C.

_ _ _ _ _ _ _ _ _

D.

_ _ _ _ _ _ _ _ _

E.

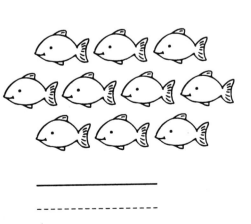

_ _ _ _ _ _ _ _ _

F.

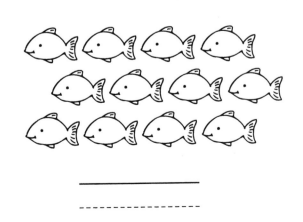

_ _ _ _ _ _ _ _ _

Name ____________________

Pretty Hats

Draw circles to show the number.

A. 7
seven

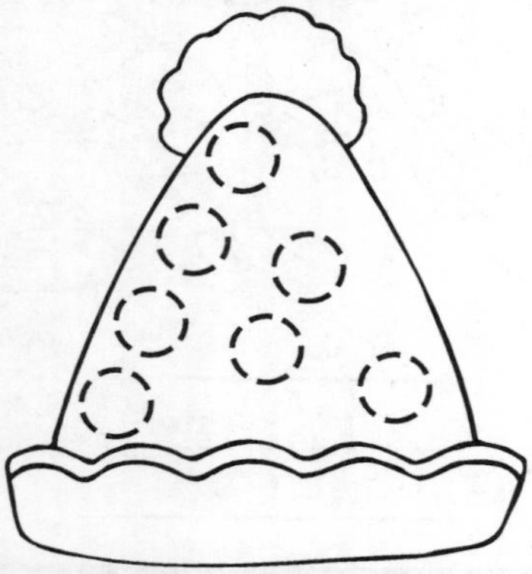

B. 8
eight

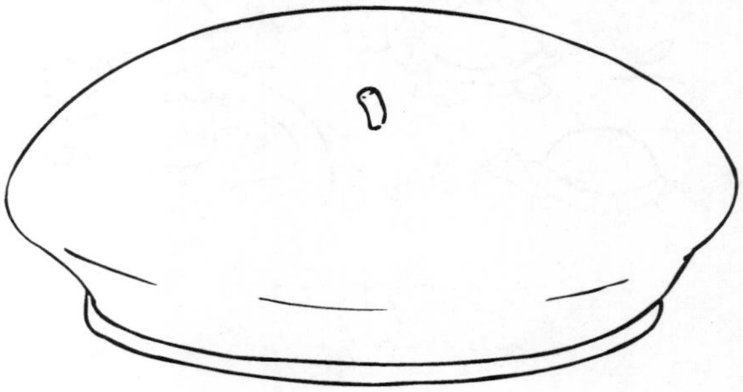

C. 9
nine

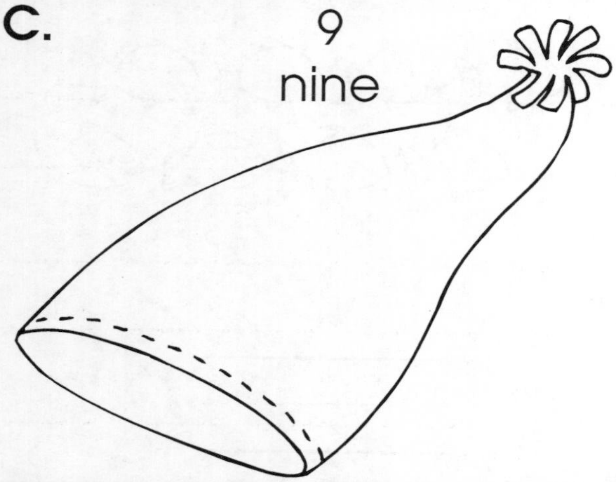

D. 10
ten

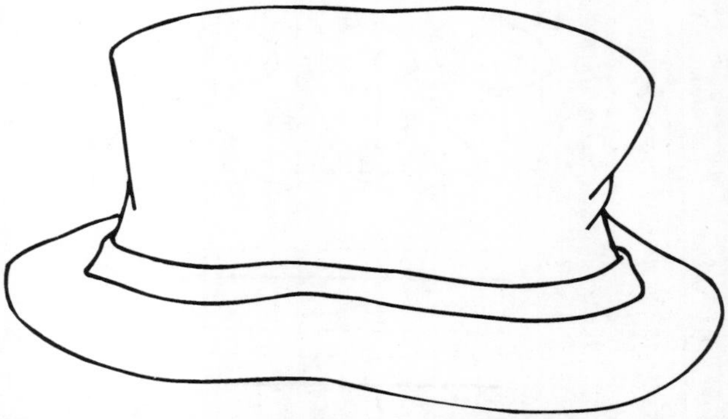

E. 11
eleven

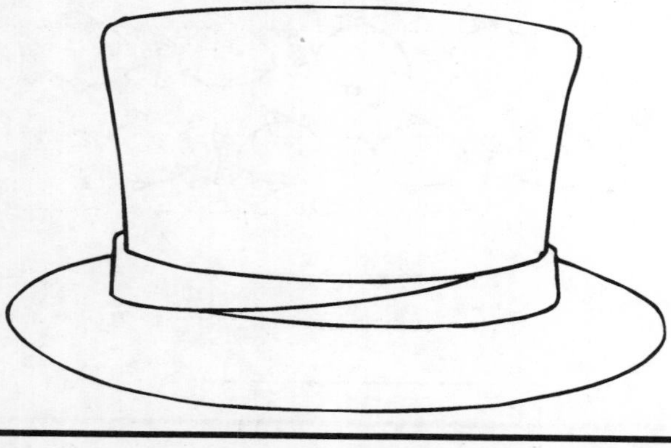

F. 12
twelve

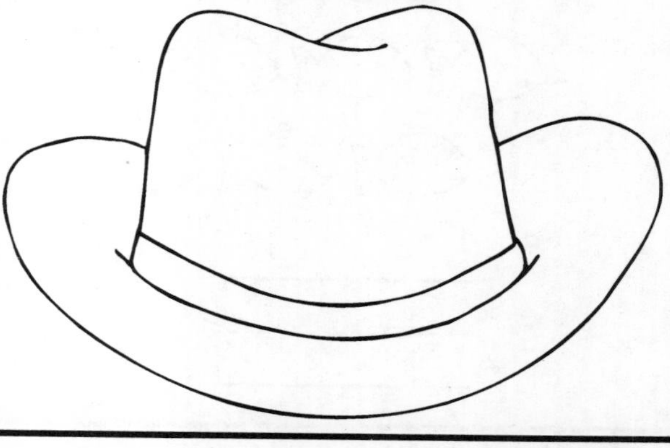

At the Park

Count. Color a box for each item. Write the number.

The Park

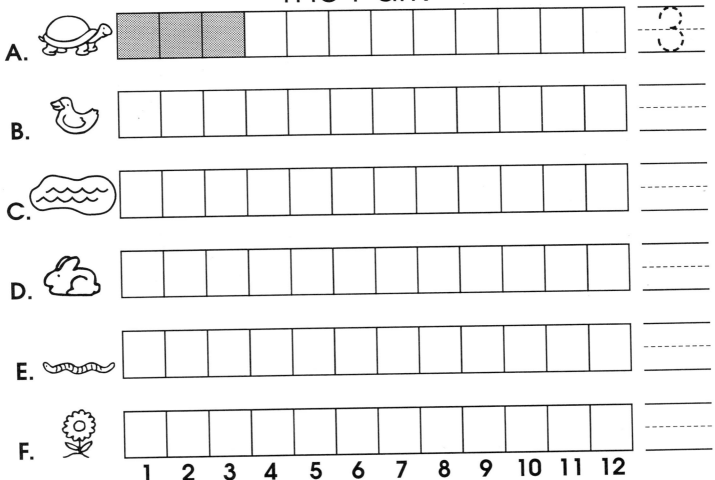

FS-32068 First Grade Math Review

A Shapely Graph

Count. Color a box for each shape. Write the number.

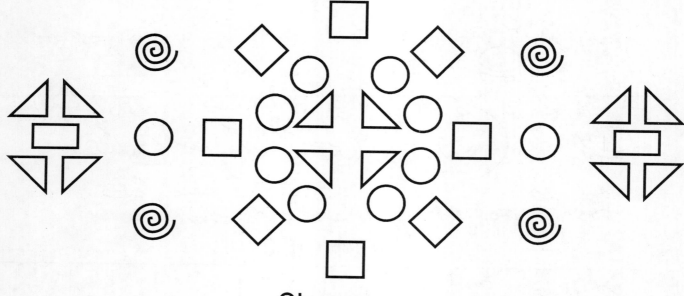

Shapes

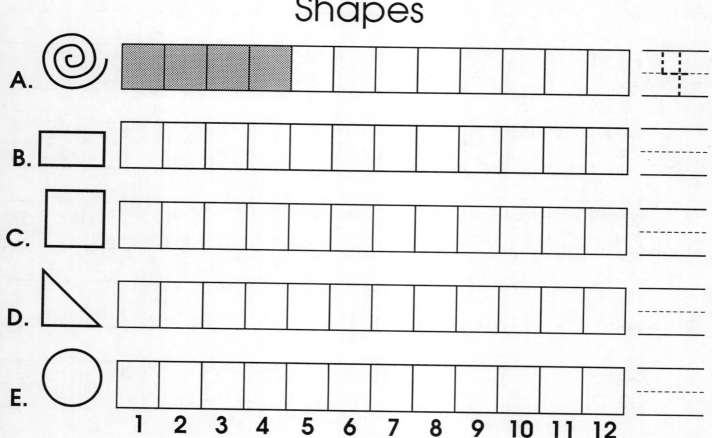

FS-32068 First Grade Math Review

Name _____

Number Express

Write the missing numbers.

A.

B.

C.

D.

E.

9

FS-32068 First Grade Math Review

What Comes Next?

Write the missing numbers.

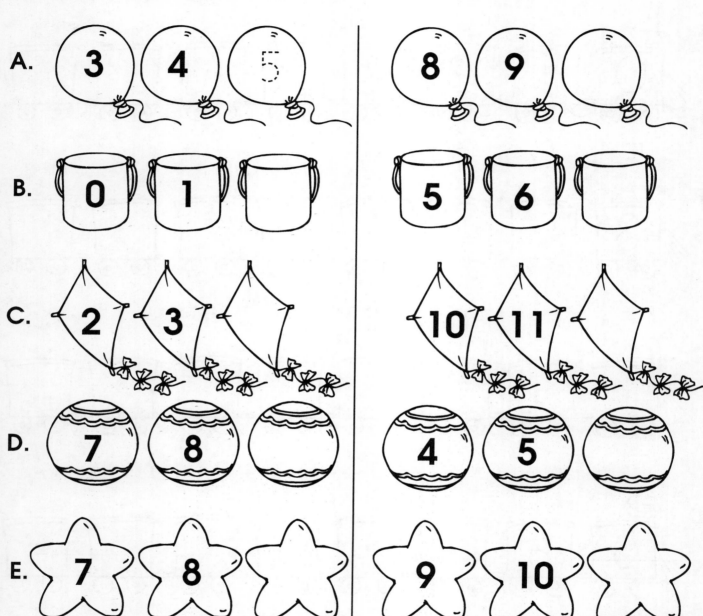

A. 3 4 5 | 8 9 ◯

B. 0 1 ◯ | 5 6 ◯

C. 2 3 ◯ | 10 11 ◯

D. 7 8 ◯ | 4 5 ◯

E. 7 8 ◯ | 9 10 ◯

Count backwards. Write the missing numbers.

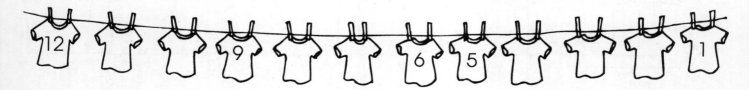

12 _ _ 9 _ _ 6 5 _ _ 1

FS-32068 First Grade Math Review

Sea Creatures

Count. Write the number. Circle the number that is greater.

A.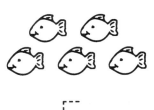

5 _____ 9 _____

B.

_____ _____

C.

_____ _____

D.

_____ _____

E.

_____ _____

F.

_____ _____

G.

_____ _____

H.

_____ _____

Bear Compare

Write which number is greater and which number is less.

A.
5
2

greater [5]   less [2]

B.
4
6

greater [ ]   less [ ]

C.
7
10

greater [ ]   less [ ]

D.
9
8

greater [ ]   less [ ]

E.
12
9

greater [ ]   less [ ]

F.
11
8

greater [ ]   less [ ]

G.
6
9

greater [ ]   less [ ]

H.
10
11

greater [ ]   less [ ]

I.
7
5

greater [ ]   less [ ]

J.
12
10

greater [ ]   less [ ]

12

Adding Apples

Draw 🍎 on the trees to show the numbers.
Write how many in all.

A.
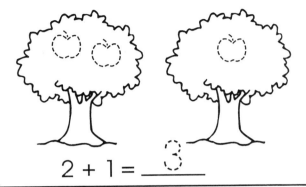
2 + 1 = ___

B.

1 + 3 = ___

C.
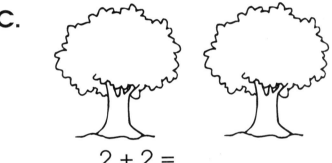
2 + 2 = ___

D.
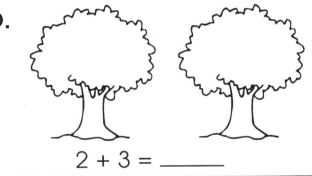
2 + 3 = ___

E.
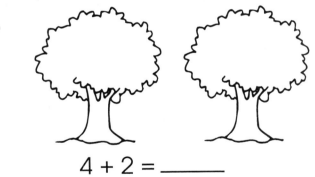
4 + 2 = ___

F.

3 + 3 = ___

G.

4 + 1 = ___

H.
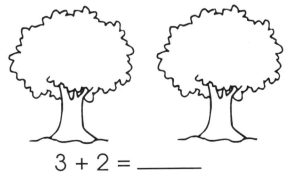
3 + 2 = ___

FS-32068 First Grade Math Review

Join in the Fun

Write the number sentence to go with the picture.

A.

___2___ + ___1___ = ___3___

B.

___ + ___ = ___

C.

___ + ___ = ___

D.

___ + ___ = ___

E.

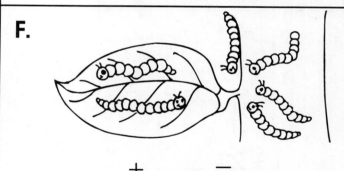

___ + ___ = ___

F.

___ + ___ = ___

G.

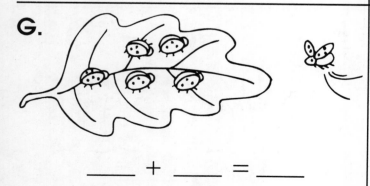

___ + ___ = ___

H.

___ + ___ = ___

FS-32068 First Grade Math Review

Name_____

Ring the Bells

Add.

A.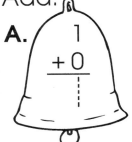
$$\begin{array}{r} 1 \\ +0 \\ \hline \end{array}$$
$$\begin{array}{r} 0 \\ +3 \\ \hline \end{array}$$

$$\begin{array}{r} 4 \\ +0 \\ \hline \end{array}$$
$$\begin{array}{r} 10 \\ +\ 0 \\ \hline \end{array}$$

$$\begin{array}{r} 0 \\ +1 \\ \hline \end{array}$$

B.
$$\begin{array}{r} 0 \\ +6 \\ \hline \end{array}$$
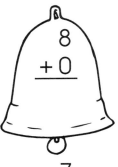
$$\begin{array}{r} 8 \\ +0 \\ \hline \end{array}$$
$$\begin{array}{r} 2 \\ +0 \\ \hline \end{array}$$

$$\begin{array}{r} 3 \\ +0 \\ \hline \end{array}$$
$$\begin{array}{r} 0 \\ +7 \\ \hline \end{array}$$

C.
$$\begin{array}{r} 3 \\ +0 \\ \hline \end{array}$$
$$\begin{array}{r} 7 \\ +0 \\ \hline \end{array}$$

$$\begin{array}{r} 0 \\ +4 \\ \hline \end{array}$$
$$\begin{array}{r} 0 \\ +2 \\ \hline \end{array}$$

$$\begin{array}{r} 0 \\ +0 \\ \hline \end{array}$$

D.
$$\begin{array}{r} 1 \\ +0 \\ \hline \end{array}$$

$$\begin{array}{r} 6 \\ +0 \\ \hline \end{array}$$
$$\begin{array}{r} 0 \\ +9 \\ \hline \end{array}$$
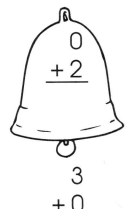
$$\begin{array}{r} 0 \\ +2 \\ \hline \end{array}$$
$$\begin{array}{r} 0 \\ +3 \\ \hline \end{array}$$

E.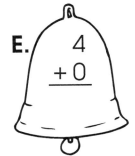
$$\begin{array}{r} 4 \\ +0 \\ \hline \end{array}$$
$$\begin{array}{r} 0 \\ +5 \\ \hline \end{array}$$

$$\begin{array}{r} 0 \\ +8 \\ \hline \end{array}$$
$$\begin{array}{r} 3 \\ +0 \\ \hline \end{array}$$

$$\begin{array}{r} 0 \\ +0 \\ \hline \end{array}$$

F.
$$\begin{array}{r} 0 \\ +10 \\ \hline \end{array}$$
$$\begin{array}{r} 0 \\ +4 \\ \hline \end{array}$$
$$\begin{array}{r} 9 \\ +0 \\ \hline \end{array}$$
$$\begin{array}{r} 5 \\ +0 \\ \hline \end{array}$$
$$\begin{array}{r} 6 \\ +0 \\ \hline \end{array}$$

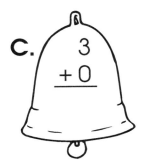

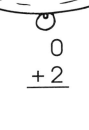

Soaring With Zero

Add.

A. 0 + 0 = _____   0 + 1 = _____

B. 0 + 3 = _____   9 + 0 = _____

C. 2 + 0 = _____   8 + 0 = _____   5 + 0 = _____

D. 0 + 7 = _____   0 + 6 = _____   1 + 0 = _____

E. 3 + 0 = _____   10 + 0 = _____   0 + 2 = _____

F. 4 + 0 = _____   6 + 0 = _____   0 + 8 = _____

G. 7 + 0 = _____   0 + 9 = _____   0 + 5 = _____

H. 0 + 4 = _____   0 + 0 = _____   6 + 0 = _____

I. 0 + 9 = _____   3 + 0 = _____   8 + 0 = _____

Write the number sentence.

J.

_____ + _____ = _____   _____ + _____ = _____

Name_____

Baskets of Eggs

Draw the eggs in each basket. Write how many in all.

A.

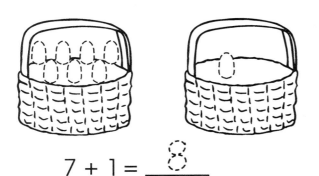

$7 + 1 =$ _____ 8

B.

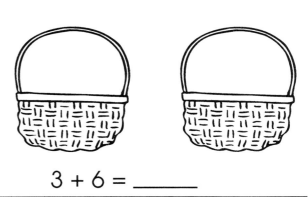

$3 + 6 =$ _____

C.

$8 + 2 =$ _____

D.

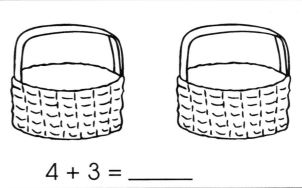

$4 + 3 =$ _____

E.

$5 + 2 =$ _____

F.

$4 + 5 =$ _____

G.

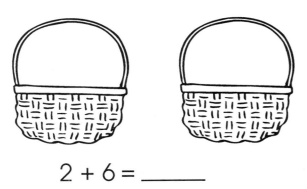

$2 + 6 =$ _____

H.

$5 + 5 =$ _____

19

Animal Addition

Write the number sentence to go with the picture.

A.

$\underline{3} + \underline{7} = \underline{10}$

B.

___ + ___ = ___

C.
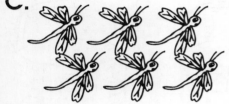

___ + ___ = ___

D.
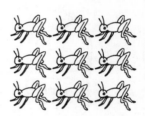

___ + ___ = ___

E.

___ + ___ = ___

F.

___ + ___ = ___

G.

___ + ___ = ___

H.

___ + ___ = ___

Bubblegum Fun

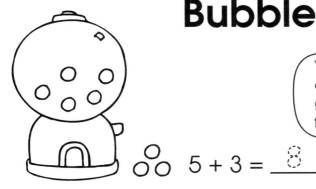

You can count on to add. Start with **5** gumballs. Count on— **five** . . . six, seven, **eight**.

$5 + 3 = 8$

Count on to add.

A.

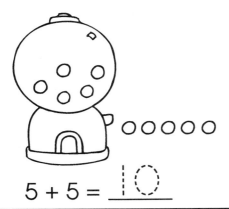

$5 + 5 = 10$

B.

$7 + 3 = $ _____

C.

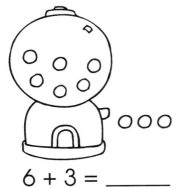

$6 + 3 = $ _____

D.

$3 + 4 = $ _____

E.

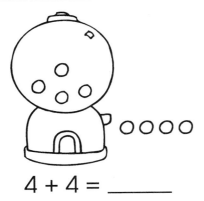

$4 + 4 = $ _____

F.

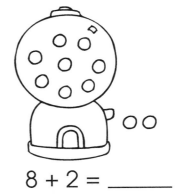

$8 + 2 = $ _____

FS-32068 First Grade Math Review

Name _____

Bunny Hop

Start at **6**. Then count on 2 more spaces—**six** . . . seven, **eight**.

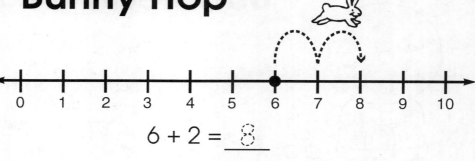

$6 + 2 = \underline{8}$

Use the number line to count on. Write the sums.

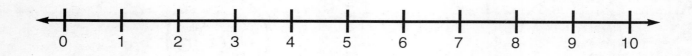

A. $4 + 3 = \underline{7}$ $5 + 2 = \underline{}$ $4 + 2 = \underline{}$

B. $6 + 1 = \underline{}$ $5 + 3 = \underline{}$ $7 + 2 = \underline{}$

C. $8 + 1 = \underline{}$ $9 + 0 = \underline{}$ $6 + 2 = \underline{}$

D. $5 + 4 = \underline{}$ $8 + 2 = \underline{}$ $7 + 3 = \underline{}$

E. $6 + 3 = \underline{}$ $9 + 1 = \underline{}$ $10 + 0 = \underline{}$

F. $5 + 5 = \underline{}$ $3 + 2 = \underline{}$ $6 + 4 = \underline{}$

G. $8 + 0 = \underline{}$ $7 + 1 = \underline{}$ $3 + 3 = \underline{}$

     FS-32068 First Grade Math Review

Domino Dots

Look at the domino. Switch the order of the dots. Write the number sentence. Add.

A.  $2 + 3 = 5$

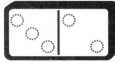 $3 + 2 = 5$

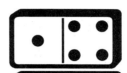 $1 + 4 = \underline{\ \ }$

$\underline{\ \ } + \underline{\ \ } = \underline{\ \ }$

B.  $4 + 3 = \underline{\ \ }$

$\underline{\ \ } + \underline{\ \ } = \underline{\ \ }$

 $5 + 2 = \underline{\ \ }$

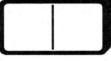 $\underline{\ \ } + \underline{\ \ } = \underline{\ \ }$

C.  $3 + 5 = \underline{\ \ }$

 $\underline{\ \ } + \underline{\ \ } = \underline{\ \ }$

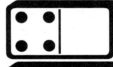 $4 + 0 = \underline{\ \ }$

 $\underline{\ \ } + \underline{\ \ } = \underline{\ \ }$

D.  $5 + 1 = \underline{\ \ }$

 $\underline{\ \ } + \underline{\ \ } = \underline{\ \ }$

 $2 + 4 = \underline{\ \ }$

 $\underline{\ \ } + \underline{\ \ } = \underline{\ \ }$

E.  $2 + 6 = \underline{\ \ }$

 $\underline{\ \ } + \underline{\ \ } = \underline{\ \ }$

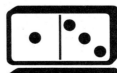 $1 + 3 = \underline{\ \ }$

 $\underline{\ \ } + \underline{\ \ } = \underline{\ \ }$

Catch a Match

Add. Match the number sentences that have the same addends.

A. 4 + 2 = __6__ •   • 1 + 4 = _____

B. 3 + 5 = _____ •   • 2 + 4 = __6__

C. 4 + 1 = _____ •   • 3 + 2 = _____

D. 2 + 3 = _____ •   • 3 + 4 = _____

E. 5 + 2 = _____ •   • 5 + 3 = _____

F. 4 + 3 = _____ •   • 2 + 5 = _____

G. 1 + 3 = _____ •   • 3 + 1 = _____

H. 4 + 5 = _____ •   • 1 + 5 = _____

I. 3 + 6 = _____ •   • 2 + 6 = _____

J. 7 + 3 = _____ •   • 5 + 4 = _____

K. 5 + 1 = _____ •   • 6 + 3 = _____

L. 6 + 2 = _____ •   • 3 + 7 = _____

Name_____

School Time

Draw more pictures to fill in the squares.
Complete the number sentence.

A.
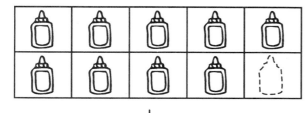
9 + ___ = 10

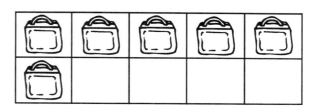
6 + ___ = 10

B.
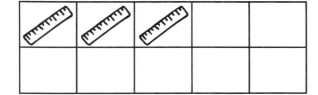
7 + ___ = 10

5 + ___ = 10

C.
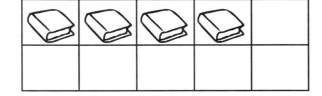
3 + ___ = 10

8 + ___ = 10

D.
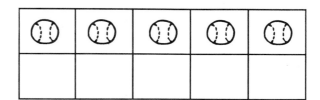
4 + ___ = 10

2 + ___ = 10

Find the Missing Numbers

Write the missing number.

A.
$$6 + \boxed{3} = 9$$
$$5 + \boxed{} = 8$$
$$4 + \boxed{} = 6$$
$$2 + \boxed{} = 9$$

B.
$$9 + \boxed{} = 10$$
$$8 + \boxed{} = 10$$
$$7 + \boxed{} = 8$$
$$3 + \boxed{} = 5$$

C.
$$5 + \boxed{} = 9$$
$$3 + \boxed{} = 7$$
$$2 + \boxed{} = 5$$
$$2 + \boxed{} = 4$$
$$10 + \boxed{} = 10$$
$$5 + \boxed{} = 6$$

D.
$$5 + \boxed{} = 7$$
$$6 + \boxed{} = 10$$
$$7 + \boxed{} = 9$$
$$9 + \boxed{} = 9$$
$$8 + \boxed{} = 8$$
$$4 + \boxed{} = 7$$

E.
$$3 + \boxed{} = 6$$
$$2 + \boxed{} = 6$$
$$5 + \boxed{} = 10$$
$$4 + \boxed{} = 7$$
$$3 + \boxed{} = 10$$
$$4 + \boxed{} = 5$$

F.
$$7 + \boxed{} = 10$$
$$4 + \boxed{} = 7$$
$$6 + \boxed{} = 7$$
$$7 + \boxed{} = 10$$
$$2 + \boxed{} = 8$$
$$6 + \boxed{} = 6$$

FS-32068 First Grade Math Review

Name_____

Cross It Out

Cross out (**X**) the pictures.
Write how many are left.

A.

$3 - 1 = \underline{}2$

B.

$5 - 2 = \underline{}$

C.

$4 - 2 = \underline{}$

D.

$5 - 1 = \underline{}$

E.

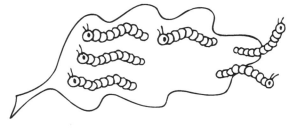

$6 - 2 = \underline{}$

F.

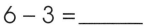

$6 - 3 = \underline{}$

G.

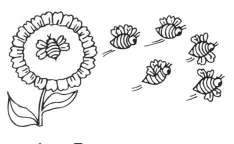

$6 - 5 = \underline{}$

H.

$5 - 3 = \underline{}$

FS-32068 First Grade Math Review

Name _____

Watch for Falling Apples

Write a number sentence to go with the picture.

A.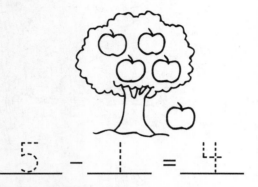

5 - 1 = 4

B.

_____ - _____ = _____

C.

_____ - _____ = _____

D.

_____ - _____ = _____

E.

_____ - _____ = _____

F.

_____ - _____ = _____

G.

_____ - _____ = _____

H.

_____ - _____ = _____

28

Name _____

A Subtraction Race

Subtract.

A. $3 - 1 = \underline{2}$ $2 - 1 = \underline{\hspace{1cm}}$

B. $3 - 2 = \underline{\hspace{1cm}}$ $4 - 1 = \underline{\hspace{1cm}}$

C. $5 - 2 = \underline{\hspace{1cm}}$ $5 - 3 = \underline{\hspace{1cm}}$ $6 - 1 = \underline{\hspace{1cm}}$

D. $4 - 2 = \underline{\hspace{1cm}}$ $6 - 4 = \underline{\hspace{1cm}}$ $4 - 3 = \underline{\hspace{1cm}}$

E. $6 - 5 = \underline{\hspace{1cm}}$ $5 - 1 = \underline{\hspace{1cm}}$ $5 - 4 = \underline{\hspace{1cm}}$

F. $6 - 2 = \underline{\hspace{1cm}}$ $3 - 1 = \underline{\hspace{1cm}}$ $6 - 4 = \underline{\hspace{1cm}}$

G. $5 - 3 = \underline{\hspace{1cm}}$ $5 - 2 = \underline{\hspace{1cm}}$ $4 - 2 = \underline{\hspace{1cm}}$

H. $2 - 1 = \underline{\hspace{1cm}}$ $6 - 3 = \underline{\hspace{1cm}}$ $6 - 5 = \underline{\hspace{1cm}}$

I. $3 - 2 = \underline{\hspace{1cm}}$ $5 - 1 = \underline{\hspace{1cm}}$ $6 - 2 = \underline{\hspace{1cm}}$

J. $4 - 3 = \underline{\hspace{1cm}}$ $5 - 4 = \underline{\hspace{1cm}}$ $3 - 2 = \underline{\hspace{1cm}}$

K. $4 - 1 = \underline{\hspace{1cm}}$ $6 - 5 = \underline{\hspace{1cm}}$ $5 - 2 = \underline{\hspace{1cm}}$

L. $6 - 1 = \underline{\hspace{1cm}}$ $6 - 3 = \underline{\hspace{1cm}}$ $5 - 3 = \underline{\hspace{1cm}}$

Away We Go!

Subtract.

A. $\begin{array}{r} 2 \\ -1 \\ \hline \end{array}$ $\begin{array}{r} 4 \\ -3 \\ \hline \end{array}$ $\begin{array}{r} 3 \\ -2 \\ \hline \end{array}$ $\begin{array}{r} 6 \\ -3 \\ \hline \end{array}$ $\begin{array}{r} 3 \\ -1 \\ \hline \end{array}$

B. $\begin{array}{r} 4 \\ -1 \\ \hline \end{array}$ $\begin{array}{r} 5 \\ -3 \\ \hline \end{array}$ $\begin{array}{r} 5 \\ -4 \\ \hline \end{array}$ $\begin{array}{r} 4 \\ -3 \\ \hline \end{array}$ $\begin{array}{r} 5 \\ -2 \\ \hline \end{array}$ $\begin{array}{r} 4 \\ -2 \\ \hline \end{array}$ $\begin{array}{r} 3 \\ -1 \\ \hline \end{array}$ $\begin{array}{r} 6 \\ -2 \\ \hline \end{array}$

C. $\begin{array}{r} 5 \\ -1 \\ \hline \end{array}$ $\begin{array}{r} 6 \\ -2 \\ \hline \end{array}$ $\begin{array}{r} 5 \\ -2 \\ \hline \end{array}$ $\begin{array}{r} 3 \\ -2 \\ \hline \end{array}$ $\begin{array}{r} 6 \\ -1 \\ \hline \end{array}$ $\begin{array}{r} 6 \\ -4 \\ \hline \end{array}$ $\begin{array}{r} 4 \\ -3 \\ \hline \end{array}$ $\begin{array}{r} 5 \\ -2 \\ \hline \end{array}$

D. $\begin{array}{r} 6 \\ -1 \\ \hline \end{array}$ $\begin{array}{r} 2 \\ -1 \\ \hline \end{array}$ $\begin{array}{r} 6 \\ -3 \\ \hline \end{array}$ $\begin{array}{r} 2 \\ -1 \\ \hline \end{array}$ $\begin{array}{r} 4 \\ -2 \\ \hline \end{array}$ $\begin{array}{r} 3 \\ -2 \\ \hline \end{array}$ $\begin{array}{r} 6 \\ -5 \\ \hline \end{array}$ $\begin{array}{r} 4 \\ -3 \\ \hline \end{array}$

E. $\begin{array}{r} 3 \\ -2 \\ \hline \end{array}$ $\begin{array}{r} 4 \\ -1 \\ \hline \end{array}$ $\begin{array}{r} 5 \\ -3 \\ \hline \end{array}$ $\begin{array}{r} 6 \\ -3 \\ \hline \end{array}$ $\begin{array}{r} 6 \\ -5 \\ \hline \end{array}$ $\begin{array}{r} 4 \\ -2 \\ \hline \end{array}$ $\begin{array}{r} 6 \\ -1 \\ \hline \end{array}$ $\begin{array}{r} 5 \\ -4 \\ \hline \end{array}$

F. $\begin{array}{r} 5 \\ -4 \\ \hline \end{array}$ $\begin{array}{r} 3 \\ -1 \\ \hline \end{array}$ $\begin{array}{r} 6 \\ -3 \\ \hline \end{array}$ $\begin{array}{r} 6 \\ -2 \\ \hline \end{array}$ $\begin{array}{r} 5 \\ -1 \\ \hline \end{array}$ $\begin{array}{r} 6 \\ -4 \\ \hline \end{array}$ $\begin{array}{r} 5 \\ -2 \\ \hline \end{array}$ $\begin{array}{r} 5 \\ -3 \\ \hline \end{array}$

    FS-32068 First Grade Math Review

Busy Bees

Subtract.

A.
$$\begin{array}{r} 1 \\ -0 \\ \hline \end{array}$$
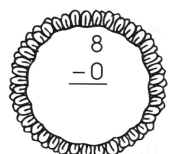
$$\begin{array}{r} 3 \\ -3 \\ \hline \end{array}$$
$$\begin{array}{r} 6 \\ -0 \\ \hline \end{array}$$
$$\begin{array}{r} 8 \\ -0 \\ \hline \end{array}$$

B.
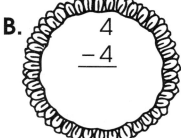
$$\begin{array}{r} 4 \\ -4 \\ \hline \end{array}$$
$$\begin{array}{r} 2 \\ -0 \\ \hline \end{array}$$
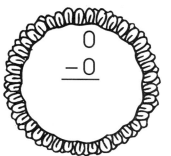
$$\begin{array}{r} 0 \\ -0 \\ \hline \end{array}$$
$$\begin{array}{r} 7 \\ -7 \\ \hline \end{array}$$

C.
$$\begin{array}{r} 2 \\ -2 \\ \hline \end{array}$$

$$\begin{array}{r} 6 \\ -6 \\ \hline \end{array}$$
$$\begin{array}{r} 9 \\ -0 \\ \hline \end{array}$$
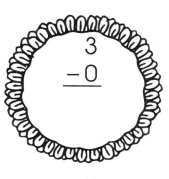
$$\begin{array}{r} 3 \\ -0 \\ \hline \end{array}$$

D.
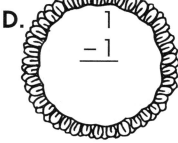
$$\begin{array}{r} 1 \\ -1 \\ \hline \end{array}$$
$$\begin{array}{r} 5 \\ -0 \\ \hline \end{array}$$
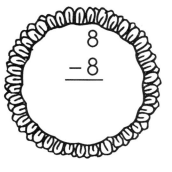
$$\begin{array}{r} 8 \\ -8 \\ \hline \end{array}$$
$$\begin{array}{r} 5 \\ -5 \\ \hline \end{array}$$

E.
$$\begin{array}{r} 4 \\ -0 \\ \hline \end{array}$$
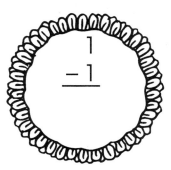
$$\begin{array}{r} 1 \\ -1 \\ \hline \end{array}$$
$$\begin{array}{r} 7 \\ -0 \\ \hline \end{array}$$
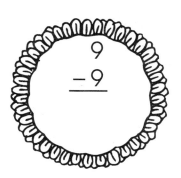
$$\begin{array}{r} 9 \\ -9 \\ \hline \end{array}$$

FS-32068 First Grade Math Review

Full or Empty?

Subtract.

A.

0 – 0 = _____

4 – 0 = _____

8 – 0 = _____

6 – 6 = _____

3 – 3 = _____

B.

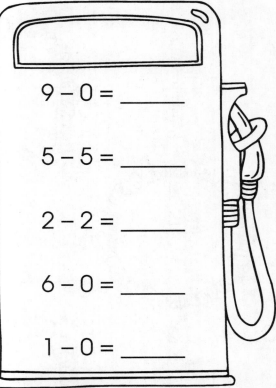

9 – 0 = _____

5 – 5 = _____

2 – 2 = _____

6 – 0 = _____

1 – 0 = _____

C.

9 – 9 = _____

7 – 0 = _____

4 – 4 = _____

1 – 1 = _____

3 – 0 = _____

D.

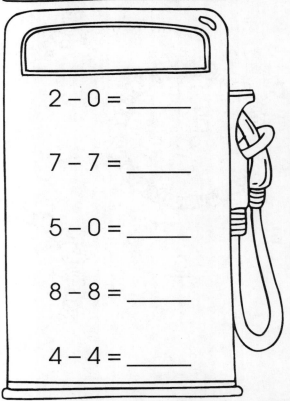

2 – 0 = _____

7 – 7 = _____

5 – 0 = _____

8 – 8 = _____

4 – 4 = _____

Leap Frog

Start at **8**. Count back 2 spaces— **eight** . . . seven, **six**.

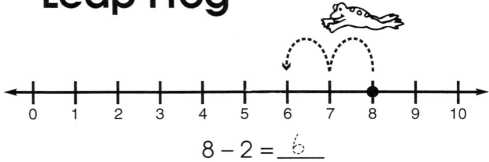

$$8 - 2 = \underline{6}$$

Use the number line to count back. Write the differences.

A. $7 - 2 = \underline{5}$ $6 - 1 = \underline{\hspace{1cm}}$ $8 - 3 = \underline{\hspace{1cm}}$

B. $9 - 3 = \underline{\hspace{1cm}}$ $7 - 1 = \underline{\hspace{1cm}}$ $10 - 1 = \underline{\hspace{1cm}}$

C. $8 - 1 = \underline{\hspace{1cm}}$ $9 - 0 = \underline{\hspace{1cm}}$ $10 - 3 = \underline{\hspace{1cm}}$

D. $9 - 2 = \underline{\hspace{1cm}}$ $7 - 3 = \underline{\hspace{1cm}}$ $6 - 2 = \underline{\hspace{1cm}}$

E. $10 - 2 = \underline{\hspace{1cm}}$ $9 - 4 = \underline{\hspace{1cm}}$ $7 - 0 = \underline{\hspace{1cm}}$

F. $8 - 2 = \underline{\hspace{1cm}}$ $7 - 4 = \underline{\hspace{1cm}}$ $8 - 5 = \underline{\hspace{1cm}}$

G. $8 - 4 = \underline{\hspace{1cm}}$ $10 - 0 = \underline{\hspace{1cm}}$ $6 - 3 = \underline{\hspace{1cm}}$

Lift Off!

Subtract.

A.
6	7	8	9	5	10
−3	−2	−1	−2	−3	− 6

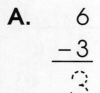

B.
10	8	6	7	7	8
− 2	−3	−2	−0	−4	−6

C.
5	7	10	9	9	10
−1	−3	− 4	−1	−7	− 9

D.
6	8	9	10	4	6
−4	−2	−3	− 1	−2	−5

E.
10	9	7	8	9	8
− 3	−4	−1	−0	−6	−5

F.
10	8	6	9	7	10
− 5	−4	−0	−5	−5	− 8

34   FS-32068 First Grade Math Review

Find the Number

Write the missing number.

A.
$$6 - \boxed{2} = 4 \qquad 7 - \boxed{} = 6 \qquad 8 - \boxed{} = 8 \qquad 5 - \boxed{} = 2 \qquad 6 - \boxed{} = 5 \qquad 8 - \boxed{} = 8$$

B.
$$5 - \boxed{} = 3 \qquad 9 - \boxed{} = 8 \qquad 10 - \boxed{} = 8 \qquad 9 - \boxed{} = 0 \qquad 4 - \boxed{} = 2 \qquad 9 - \boxed{} = 4$$

C.
$$6 - \boxed{} = 3 \qquad 8 - \boxed{} = 7 \qquad 9 - \boxed{} = 7 \qquad 7 - \boxed{} = 7 \qquad 5 - \boxed{} = 5 \qquad 4 - \boxed{} = 1$$

D.
$$10 - \boxed{} = 9 \qquad 9 - \boxed{} = 9 \qquad 7 - \boxed{} = 4 \qquad 8 - \boxed{} = 6 \qquad 6 - \boxed{} = 0 \qquad 10 - \boxed{} = 4$$

E.
$$5 - \boxed{} = 0 \qquad 10 - \boxed{} = 6 \qquad 8 - \boxed{} = 5 \qquad 7 - \boxed{} = 2$$

F.
$$9 - \boxed{} = 6 \qquad 6 - \boxed{} = 2 \qquad 8 - \boxed{} = 4 \qquad 10 - \boxed{} = 7$$

FS-32068 First Grade Math Review

Surprise!

Subtract.

A.

Subtract 1	
9	8
5	
6	
10	
7	

Subtract 3	
10	
6	
4	
8	
9	

Subtract 0	
6	
8	
9	
7	
3	

Subtract 2	
8	
9	
10	
5	
7	

B.

Subtract 2	
10	
7	
8	
6	
9	

Subtract 5	
5	
7	
6	
9	
10	

Subtract 6	
10	
6	
7	
9	
8	

Subtract 4	
10	
7	
8	
6	
9	

C.

Subtract 7	
8	
10	
9	
7	

Subtract 1	
4	
2	
3	
1	

Subtract 2	
6	
3	
4	
2	

All in the Family

Complete each fact family. Add or subtract.

A.

$1 + 5 = \underline{6}$
$5 + 1 = \underline{6}$
$6 - 1 = \underline{5}$
$6 - 5 = \underline{1}$

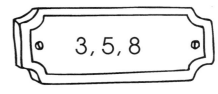

$2 + 7 = \underline{\hspace{1cm}}$
$7 + 2 = \underline{\hspace{1cm}}$
$9 - 2 = \underline{\hspace{1cm}}$
$9 - 7 = \underline{\hspace{1cm}}$

3, 5, 8

$3 + 5 = \underline{\hspace{1cm}}$
$5 + 3 = \underline{\hspace{1cm}}$
$8 - 3 = \underline{\hspace{1cm}}$
$8 - 5 = \underline{\hspace{1cm}}$

B.

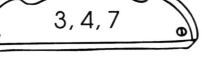

$3 + 4 = \underline{\hspace{1cm}}$
$4 + 3 = \underline{\hspace{1cm}}$
$7 - 3 = \underline{\hspace{1cm}}$
$7 - 4 = \underline{\hspace{1cm}}$

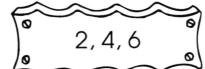

$2 + 4 = \underline{\hspace{1cm}}$
$4 + 2 = \underline{\hspace{1cm}}$
$6 - 2 = \underline{\hspace{1cm}}$
$6 - 4 = \underline{\hspace{1cm}}$

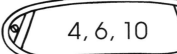

$4 + 6 = \underline{\hspace{1cm}}$
$6 + 4 = \underline{\hspace{1cm}}$
$10 - 4 = \underline{\hspace{1cm}}$
$10 - 6 = \underline{\hspace{1cm}}$

C.

3, 7, 10

$3 + 7 = \underline{\hspace{1cm}}$
$7 + 3 = \underline{\hspace{1cm}}$
$10 - 3 = \underline{\hspace{1cm}}$
$10 - 7 = \underline{\hspace{1cm}}$

$1 + 7 = \underline{\hspace{1cm}}$
$7 + 1 = \underline{\hspace{1cm}}$
$8 - 1 = \underline{\hspace{1cm}}$
$8 - 7 = \underline{\hspace{1cm}}$

$4 + 5 = \underline{\hspace{1cm}}$
$5 + 4 = \underline{\hspace{1cm}}$
$9 - 4 = \underline{\hspace{1cm}}$
$9 - 5 = \underline{\hspace{1cm}}$

Come to My House

Complete each fact family. Add or subtract.

A.

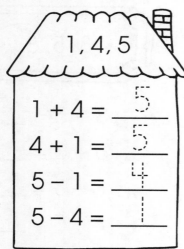

1, 4, 5

1 + 4 = 5
4 + 1 = 5
5 – 1 = 4
5 – 4 = 1

2, 5, 7

2 + 5 = ____
5 + 2 = ____
7 – 2 = ____
7 – 5 = ____

2, 6, 8

2 + 6 = ____
6 + 2 = ____
8 – 2 = ____
8 – 6 = ____

Write the number sentences for each fact family.

B.

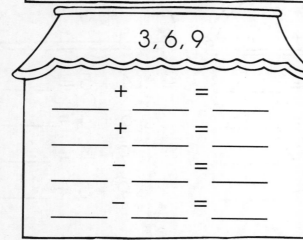

2, 4, 6

2 + 4 = 6
____ + ____ = ____
____ – ____ = ____
____ – ____ = ____

4, 6, 10

____ + ____ = ____
____ + ____ = ____
____ – ____ = ____
____ – ____ = ____

C.

3, 6, 9

____ + ____ = ____
____ + ____ = ____
____ – ____ = ____
____ – ____ = ____

2, 8, 10

____ + ____ = ____
____ + ____ = ____
____ – ____ = ____
____ – ____ = ____

FS-32068 First Grade Math Review

Balloons for You

Add or subtract. Color the balloons.

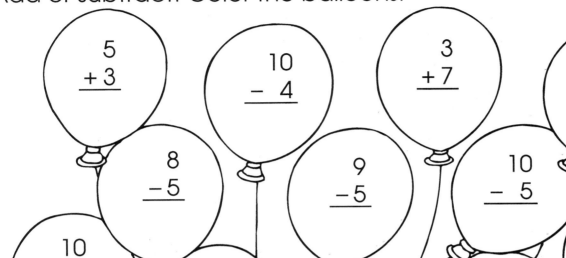

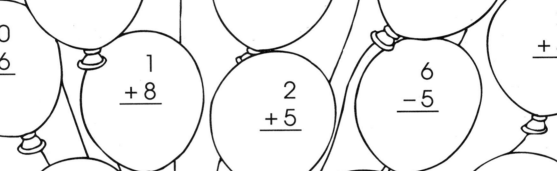

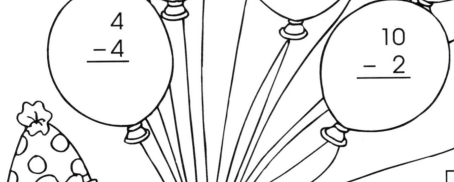

Key
0 or 1 red
2 or 3 blue
4 or 5 yellow
6 or 7 green
8 or 9 purple
10   orange

FS-32068 First Grade Math Review

Catch a Butterfly

Add or subtract.

A.
$$\begin{array}{r} 10 \\ -\ 5 \\ \hline 5 \end{array}$$
$$\begin{array}{r} 2 \\ +6 \\ \hline \end{array}$$
$$\begin{array}{r} 5 \\ +1 \\ \hline \end{array}$$
$$\begin{array}{r} 9 \\ -3 \\ \hline \end{array}$$
$$\begin{array}{r} 4 \\ +4 \\ \hline \end{array}$$
$$\begin{array}{r} 5 \\ -4 \\ \hline \end{array}$$
$$\begin{array}{r} 6 \\ -5 \\ \hline \end{array}$$

B.
$$\begin{array}{r} 7 \\ -3 \\ \hline \end{array}$$

$$\begin{array}{r} 9 \\ -6 \\ \hline \end{array}$$
$$\begin{array}{r} 10 \\ -\ 6 \\ \hline \end{array}$$
$$\begin{array}{r} 5 \\ -4 \\ \hline \end{array}$$

$$\begin{array}{r} 2 \\ +7 \\ \hline \end{array}$$

C.
$$\begin{array}{r} 3 \\ +4 \\ \hline \end{array}$$
$$\begin{array}{r} 8 \\ +2 \\ \hline \end{array}$$
$$\begin{array}{r} 6 \\ +4 \\ \hline \end{array}$$
$$\begin{array}{r} 8 \\ -2 \\ \hline \end{array}$$

$$\begin{array}{r} 4 \\ +6 \\ \hline \end{array}$$
$$\begin{array}{r} 5 \\ +5 \\ \hline \end{array}$$

D.
$$\begin{array}{r} 1 \\ +7 \\ \hline \end{array}$$
$$\begin{array}{r} 8 \\ -8 \\ \hline \end{array}$$

$$\begin{array}{r} 7 \\ +2 \\ \hline \end{array}$$
$$\begin{array}{r} 7 \\ -6 \\ \hline \end{array}$$
$$\begin{array}{r} 10 \\ -\ 8 \\ \hline \end{array}$$
$$\begin{array}{r} 5 \\ -3 \\ \hline \end{array}$$

E.
$$\begin{array}{r} 9 \\ -8 \\ \hline \end{array}$$
$$\begin{array}{r} 3 \\ +5 \\ \hline \end{array}$$
$$\begin{array}{r} 10 \\ -\ 4 \\ \hline \end{array}$$
$$\begin{array}{r} 9 \\ -7 \\ \hline \end{array}$$
$$\begin{array}{r} 9 \\ -4 \\ \hline \end{array}$$
$$\begin{array}{r} 7 \\ -5 \\ \hline \end{array}$$
$$\begin{array}{r} 6 \\ -4 \\ \hline \end{array}$$

F.
$$\begin{array}{r} 8 \\ -1 \\ \hline \end{array}$$
$$\begin{array}{r} 6 \\ +3 \\ \hline \end{array}$$
$$\begin{array}{r} 4 \\ -0 \\ \hline \end{array}$$
$$\begin{array}{r} 4 \\ +5 \\ \hline \end{array}$$
$$\begin{array}{r} 4 \\ +3 \\ \hline \end{array}$$
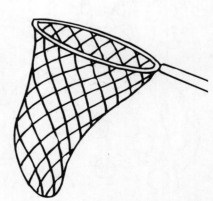

FS-32068 First Grade Math Review

Find the Solid Shape

Color each object that has the same shape.

A. 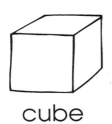 cube

B.  rectangular prism
  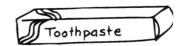

C.  cylinder

D.  cone

E.  sphere

Solids

Cross out (**X**) the shape that does not belong.

A.

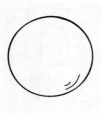
sphere

 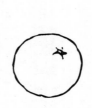 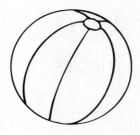

B.

cone

C.

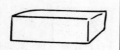
rectangular prism

D.

cylinder

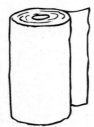   

E.

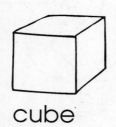
cube

Name_____

Plane Shapes

○ circle □ square △ triangle ▭ rectangle

Color the circles green.
Color the triangles red.
Color the rectangles blue.
Color the squares yellow.

FS-32068 First Grade Math Review

Name_____

How Many Can You Find?

○ circle   □ square   △ triangle   ▭ rectangle

Color the circles green.
Color the triangles red.
Color the rectangles blue.
Color the squares yellow.

Name_____

Draw a Match

Copy the shape.

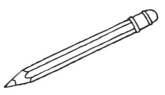

A.

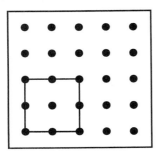 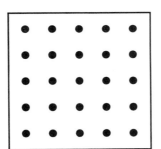

B.

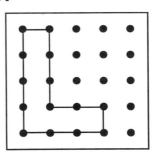 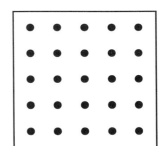

C.

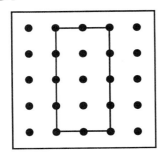 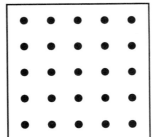

D.

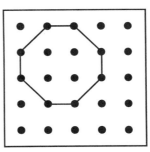 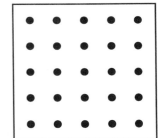

E.

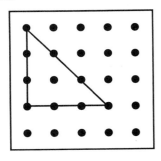 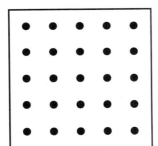

F.

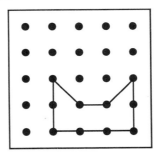 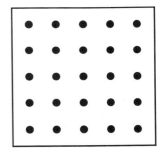

G.

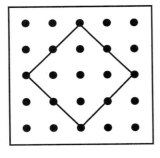 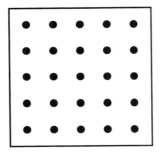

H.

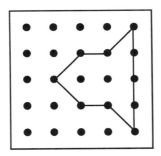 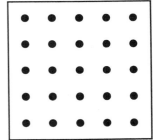

FS-32068 First Grade Math Review

A Perfect Match

In each row, color the figures that are the same size and shape.

A.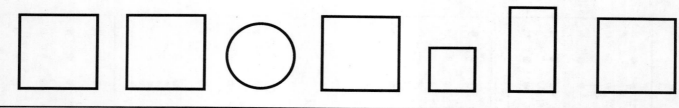

B.

C.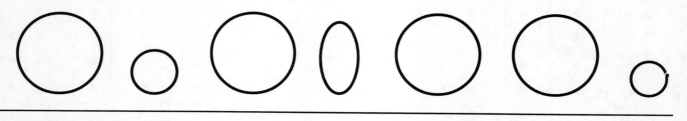

D.

E.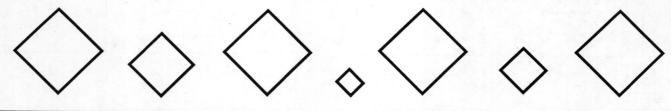

F.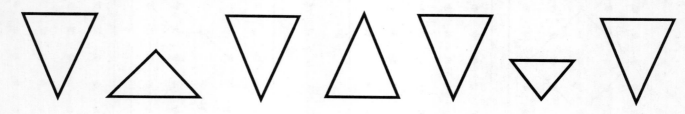

FS-32068 First Grade Math Review

Stringing Beads

Draw the next two beads in each pattern.

A.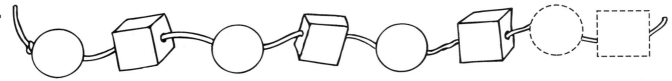

B.

C.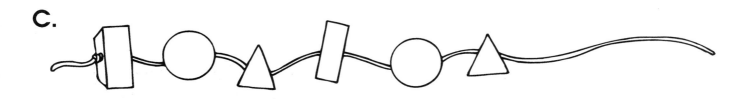

D.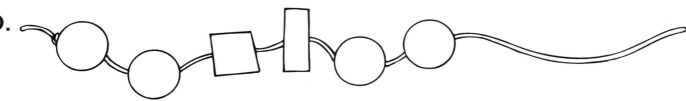

E.

F.

Name_____

Making Patterns

Draw the missing shapes.

A.

B.

C.

D.

E.

F.

FS-32068 First Grade Math Review

Name_____

Play Ball

Circle sets of ten. Write how many tens and ones.
Write the number.

A.

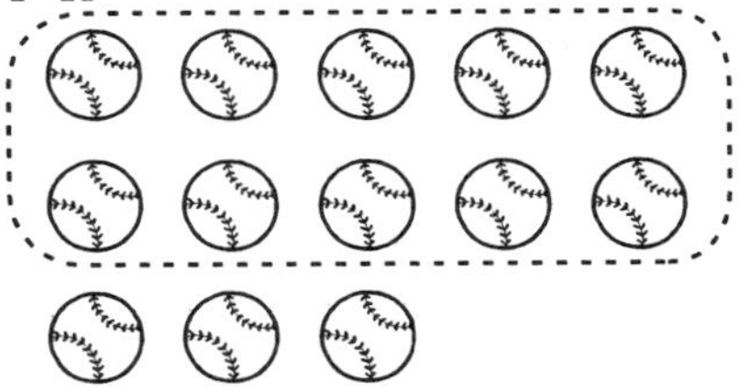

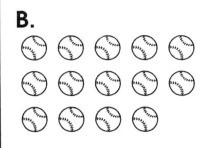

tens	ones
1	3

13

B.

tens	ones

_____

C.

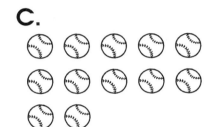

tens	ones

_____

D.

tens	ones

_____

E.

tens	ones

_____

F.

tens	ones

_____

G.

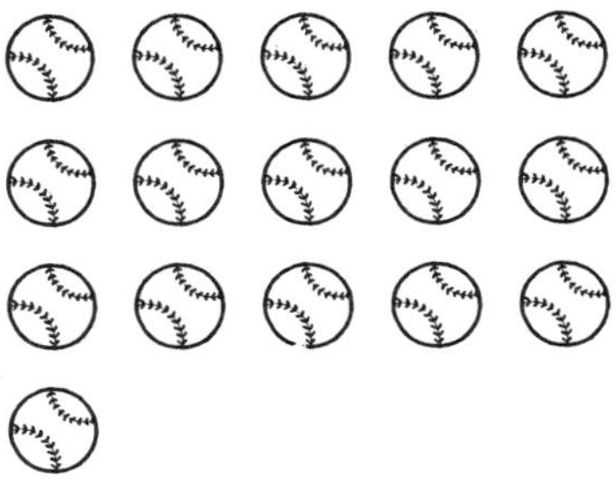

tens	ones

_____

H.

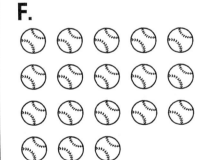

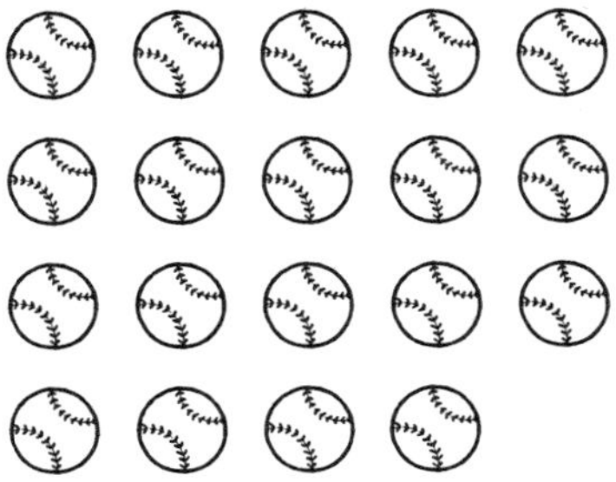

tens	ones

_____

FS-32068 First Grade Math Review

Name _____

How Many Pennies?

Circle sets of ten. Write how many tens and ones.
Write the number.

A.

tens	ones
1	4

14 ¢

B.

tens	ones

_____ ¢

C.

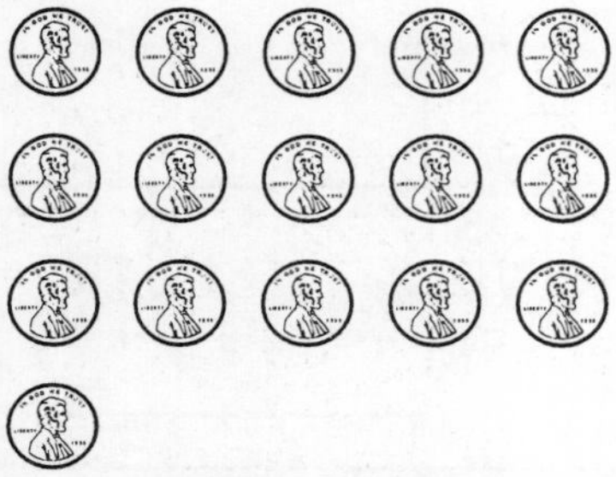

tens	ones

_____ ¢

D.

tens	ones

_____ ¢

E.

tens	ones

_____ ¢

F.

tens	ones

_____ ¢

G.

tens	ones

_____ ¢

H.

tens	ones

_____ ¢

50

Numbers to 50

Write how many tens and ones. Write the number.

A.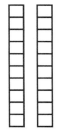

tens	ones
2	5

25

B.

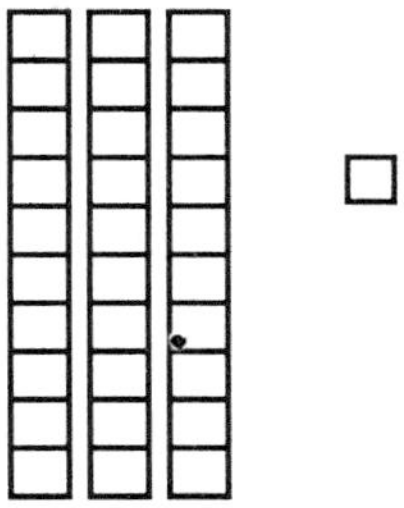

tens	ones

C.

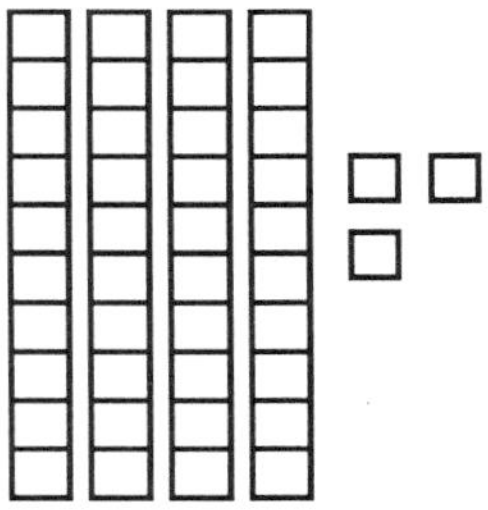

tens	ones

D.

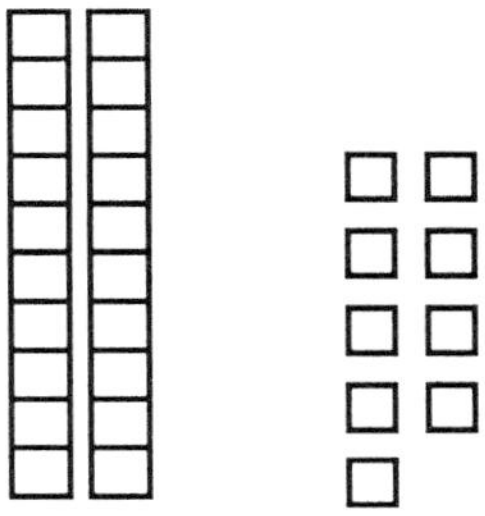

tens	ones

E.

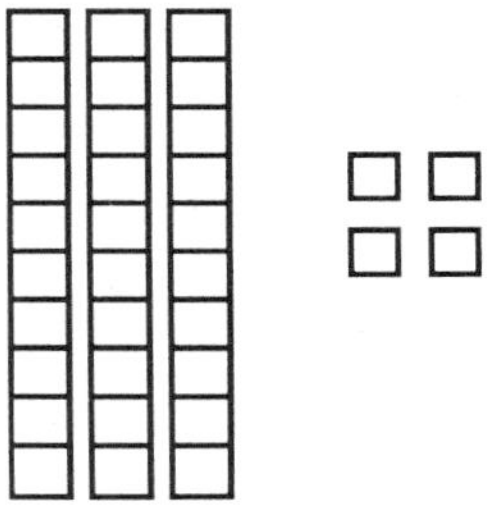

tens	ones

F.

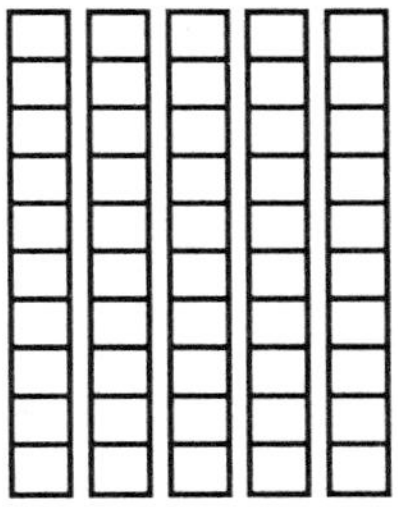

tens	ones

G.

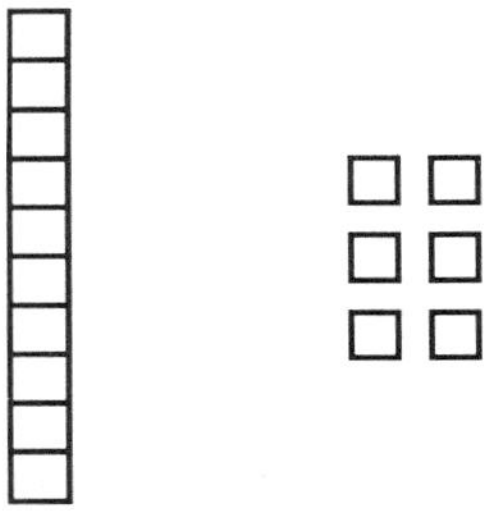

tens	ones

H.

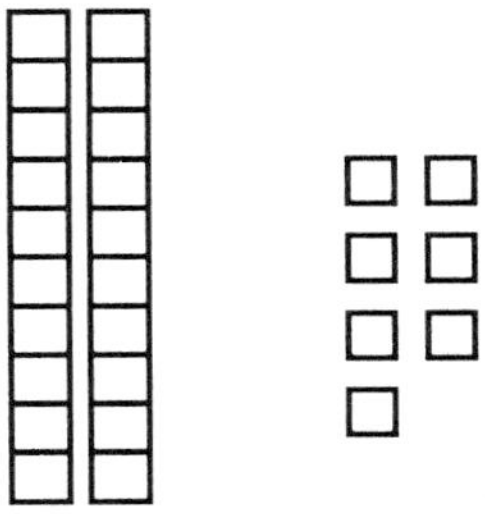

tens	ones

I. Write a number between 10 and 50.
Draw sets of tens and ones to show the number.
Write how many tens and ones.

tens	ones

_____
number

Name_____

Color the Number

Color to show the number.
Write how many tens and ones.

A. Color 23

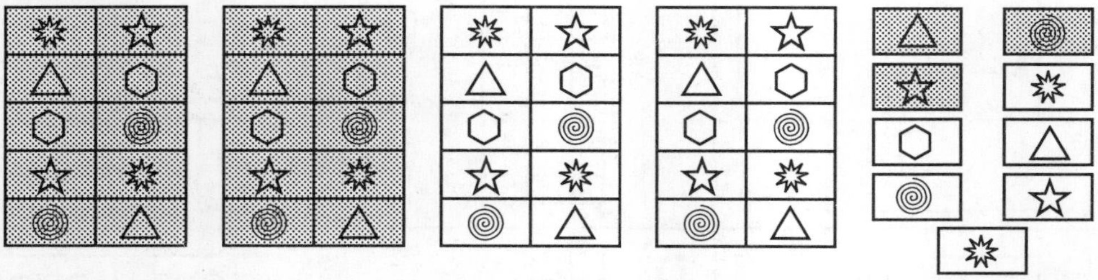

tens	ones
2	3

B. Color 42

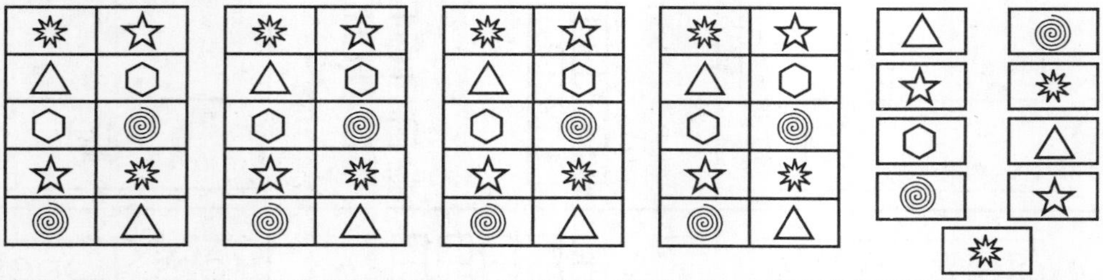

tens	ones

C. Color 36

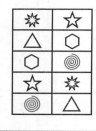

tens	ones

D. Color 21

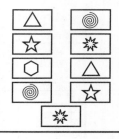

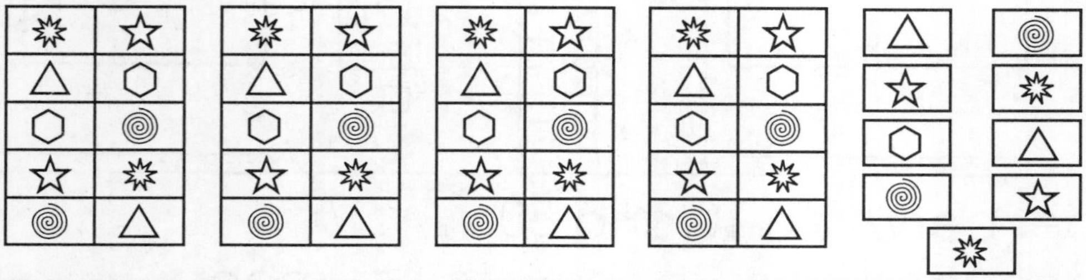

tens	ones

E. Color 15

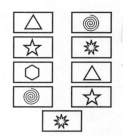

tens	ones

FS-32068 First Grade Math Review

A Hidden Path

Color the boxes from 1 to 50.
You can move left, right, up, or down.

start

1	2	8	25	49	12	13	14	15
22	3	35	9	10	11	4	21	16
13	4	28	8	36	15	24	43	17
36	5	6	7	45	21	20	19	18
12	23	36	43	23	22	37	4	14
28	27	26	25	24	18	44	45	46
29	16	9	49	12	50	43	9	47
30	10	34	35	36	15	42	19	48
31	32	33	18	37	7	41	6	49
17	8	11	20	38	39	40	15	50

end

Connect the Dots

Connect the dots from 1 to 50.

How Many Marbles?

Count. Write how many in all.

A.  56

B. 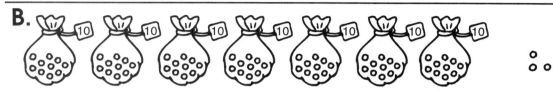 _____

C. 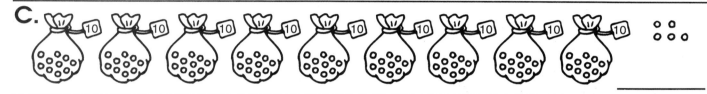 _____

D.  _____

E.  _____

F. 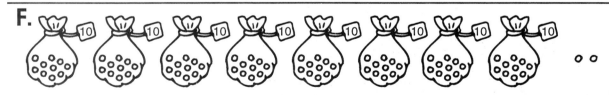 _____

G.  _____

H.  _____

FS-32068 First Grade Math Review

Count and Write

Count. Write the number that tells how many.

A.  6 4 ____

B. 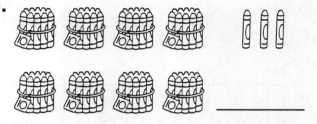 _____

C.  _____

D. 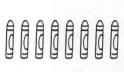 _____

E. 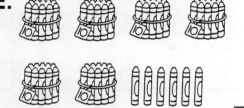 _____

F. 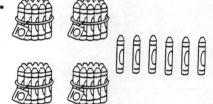 _____

G.  _____

H. 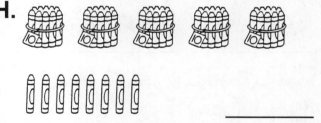 _____

I. 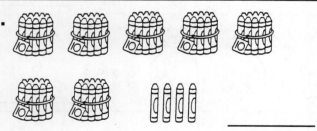 _____

J. 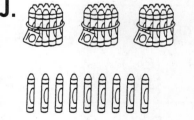 _____

K. Which number is greatest? _____

Name_____

An Elephant Joke

Write the missing numbers.

A.	25, _26_ , 27 [O]	28, 29, __ [E]	__, 32, 33 [R]
B.	__, 37, 38 [A]	39, __, 41 [E]	42, 43, __ [I]
C.	__, 71, 72 [E]	73, __, 75 [S]	76, __, 78 [W]
D.	62, __, 64 [N]	65, 66, __ [H]	__, 48, 49 [D]
E.	__, 59, 60 [R]	61, __, 63 [T]	64, __, 66 [A]
F.	86, __, 88 [S]	__, 90, 91 [E]	92, 93, __ [N]

Fill in the correct letter over each answer. Why does an elephant wear green sneakers instead of red ones?

HIS ___ ___ ___   ○ ___ ___ ___   ___ ___ ___
    31 70 47   26 94 30 74   36 58 40

___ ___   ___ ___ ___   ___ ___ ___ H.
44 63   62 67 89   77 65 87

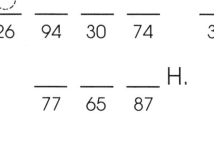

Name_____

What's Missing?

Write the missing numbers.

A.

1	2	3	4						10
	12		14						
21								29	
	32								
			45						
									60
						67			
	73								
			85						
91								99	

B. Color the numbers between 43 and 47 red.

C. Color the number that comes just after 58 blue.

D. Color the number that comes just before 90 yellow.

E. Color the number between 29 and 31 orange.

F. Color the number that comes just after 99 green.

G. Color the numbers between 71 and 75 purple.

FS-32068 First Grade Math Review

X's and O's

Look at the first number in each row.
Cross out (**X**) the numbers that are greater.
Circle the numbers that are less.

A.  (36) 7̶5̶ (29) 5̶0̶

B.    46   26   63   35

C.   74   57   80   69

D.   20   16   81   9

E.    46   63   65   70

F.    45   58   60   95

G.   19   90   83   79

H.   99   89   90   93

FS-32068 First Grade Math Review

Name ______________________ Greater than, Less than, Numeration 1–100

Building Blocks

Write two 2-digit numbers from each pair of blocks.
Circle the greater number.

A. 6 1

16 (61)

B. 4 8

_____ _____

C. 2 5

_____ _____

D. 5 3

_____ _____

E. 8 6

_____ _____

F. 1 7

_____ _____

G. 9 2

_____ _____

H. 3 4

_____ _____

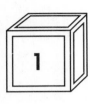

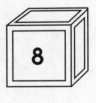

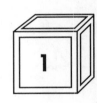

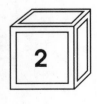

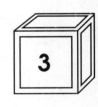

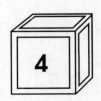

Name_____

 Skip-counting

Skip-Counting

A. Count by twos. Write the numbers.

2 __ __ __ __ __ __

B. Count by fives. Write the numbers.

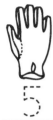

5 __ __ __ __ __ __

C. Count by tens. Write the numbers.

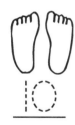

10 __ __ __ __ __ __

D. Count by tens. Connect the dots from 10 to 100.

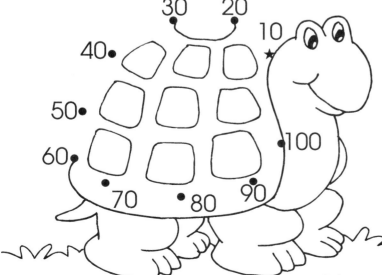 

© Frank Schaffer Publications, Inc.　61　FS-32068 First Grade Math Review

Climb the Ladders

Count by twos, fives, or tens. Write the missing numbers.

A.

2
4

10

B.

5
10

25

C.

10
20

60

D.

52
54

64

E.

16
18

24

F.

40
45

65

G.

30
40

70

H.

66
68

72

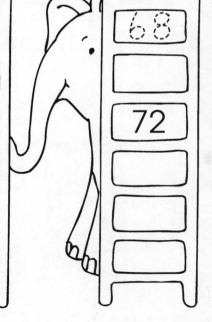

FS-32068 First Grade Math Review

Name_____

Double It

Add.

A.
4	7	1	3	2
+4	+7	+1	+3	+2

B.
0	5	6	9	8
+0	+5	+6	+9	+8

C. 4 + 4 = _____   3 + 3 = _____   7 + 7 = _____

D. 5 + 5 = _____   1 + 1 = _____   8 + 8 = _____

E. 9 + 9 = _____   2 + 2 = _____   6 + 6 = _____

Write a doubles fact for each picture.

F.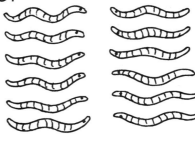

 _____ + _____ = _____   _____ + _____ = _____

63   FS-32068 First Grade Math Review

Twice as Nice

Name _____

Doubles facts, Addition facts to 18

Add.

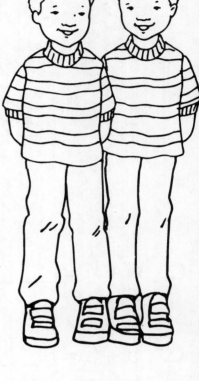

A. 4+4=8   5+5   6+6   7+7   5+5

B. 8+8   9+9   3+3   4+4   5+5

C. 9+9   0+0   2+2   1+1   7+7

Use a doubles fact to solve each riddle.

D. My double is 12. Who am I? _____

E. My double is 10. Who am I? _____

F. My double is 16. Who am I? _____

G. My double is 14. Who am I? _____

© Frank Schaffer Publications, Inc. 64 FS-32068 First Grade Math Review

Addition Wheels

Add to complete the addition wheels.

A.

Center: 5

7 | 10

2 | 5
7 | 8
4 | 3
9 | 6

B.

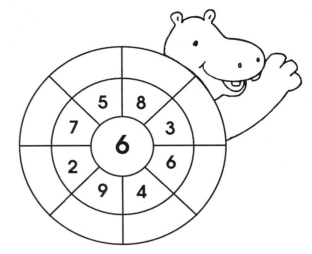

Center: 6

5 | 8
7 | 3
2 | 6
9 | 4

C.

Center: 7

7 | 8
3 | 2
4 | 5
1 | 6

D.

Center: 8

6 | 7
3 | 2
1 | 4
5 | 0

E.

Center: 4

9 | 6
2 | 1
5 | 7
3 | 8

F.

Center: 3

9 | 5
2 | 7
4 | 8
3 | 6

FS-32068 First Grade Math Review

Pop the Balloons

Add.
Color the balloons that match the sum on each dart.

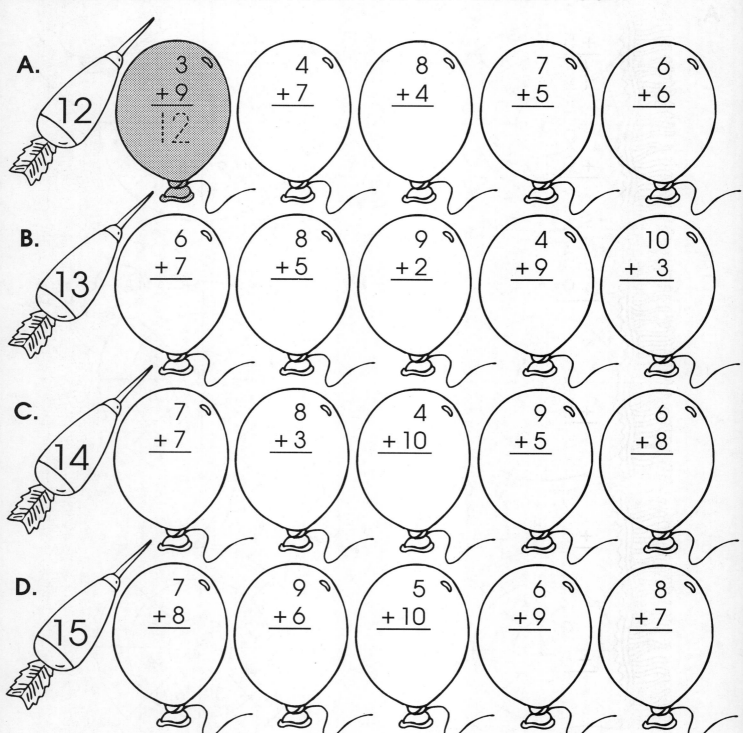

A. 12

$\begin{array}{r} 3 \\ +9 \\ \hline 12 \end{array}$ $\begin{array}{r} 4 \\ +7 \\ \hline \end{array}$ $\begin{array}{r} 8 \\ +4 \\ \hline \end{array}$ $\begin{array}{r} 7 \\ +5 \\ \hline \end{array}$ $\begin{array}{r} 6 \\ +6 \\ \hline \end{array}$

B. 13

$\begin{array}{r} 6 \\ +7 \\ \hline \end{array}$ $\begin{array}{r} 8 \\ +5 \\ \hline \end{array}$ $\begin{array}{r} 9 \\ +2 \\ \hline \end{array}$ $\begin{array}{r} 4 \\ +9 \\ \hline \end{array}$ $\begin{array}{r} 10 \\ +\ 3 \\ \hline \end{array}$

C. 14

$\begin{array}{r} 7 \\ +7 \\ \hline \end{array}$ $\begin{array}{r} 8 \\ +3 \\ \hline \end{array}$ $\begin{array}{r} 4 \\ +10 \\ \hline \end{array}$ $\begin{array}{r} 9 \\ +5 \\ \hline \end{array}$ $\begin{array}{r} 6 \\ +8 \\ \hline \end{array}$

D. 15

$\begin{array}{r} 7 \\ +8 \\ \hline \end{array}$ $\begin{array}{r} 9 \\ +6 \\ \hline \end{array}$ $\begin{array}{r} 5 \\ +10 \\ \hline \end{array}$ $\begin{array}{r} 6 \\ +9 \\ \hline \end{array}$ $\begin{array}{r} 8 \\ +7 \\ \hline \end{array}$

       FS-32068 First Grade Math Review

Magic Carpet Ride

Add.

A.

7 +5 12	4 +9	6 +5	9 +6	8 +3
9 +9	7 +4	5 +8	6 +7	8 +8

B.

8 +9	6 +6	8 +4	6 +8	7 +9
3 +8	7 +8	9 +2	5 +7	8 +6

C.

7 +7	8 +5	8 +7	5 +9	4 +7
9 +8	9 +3	6 +9	9 +4	7 +6

 FS-32068 First Grade Math Review

Double Bubble

Add.

A.	5 + 5 = 10		5 + 4 = ____		5 + 7 = ____
B.	6 + 5 = ____		5 + 0 = ____		9 + 2 = ____
C.	4 + 5 = ____		1 + 4 = ____		4 + 8 = ____
D.	4 + 3 = ____		7 + 7 = ____		5 + 6 = ____
E.	8 + 7 = ____		0 + 7 = ____		4 + 4 = ____
F.	8 + 8 = ____		8 + 5 = ____		3 + 4 = ____
G.	9 + 8 = ____		7 + 8 = ____		9 + 7 = ____
H.	7 + 9 = ____		9 + 9 = ____		10 + 4 = ____
I.	5 + 9 = ____		10 + 5 = ____		
J.	9 + 6 = ____		7 + 5 = ____		
K.	4 + 9 = ____		1 + 9 = ____		
L.	6 + 0 = ____		6 + 4 = ____		

FS-32068 First Grade Math Review

Follow the Trails

Add.

A.	9 + 9 = 18	7 + 8 = ____	8 + 6 = ____
B.	7 + 2 = ____	9 + 2 = ____	9 + 4 = ____
C.	5 + 4 = ____	10 + 6 = ____	7 + 3 = ____
D.	9 + 3 = ____	8 + 7 = ____	6 + 8 = ____
E.	5 + 5 = ____	6 + 9 = ____	8 + 2 = ____
F.	4 + 9 = ____	9 + 8 = ____	7 + 7 = ____
G.	6 + 6 = ____	5 + 9 = ____	6 + 4 = ____
H.	8 + 5 = ____	8 + 3 = ____	8 + 8 = ____
I.	5 + 6 = ____	9 + 5 = ____	5 + 8 = ____
J.	7 + 9 = ____	5 + 7 = ____	9 + 7 = ____
K.	4 + 8 = ____	7 + 4 = ____	6 + 7 = ____
L.	9 + 6 = ____	8 + 9 = ____	8 + 4 = ____

 FS-32068 First Grade Math Review

Valerie's Vine

Add.

A. 7   6   9   6   10   3
+8 +8 +3 +7 +7 +8
15

B. 9   8   5   8   6   5   7
+2 +5 +6 +9 +6 +9 +3

C. 5   8   9   9   3   4
+7 +8 +7 +9 +9 +8

D. 6   9   8   7   7   5
+9 +8 +4 +4 +9 +5

E. 9   7   8   7   6
+4 +7 +6 +5 +4

F. 8   9   7   8   8   6
+7 +6 +6 +3 +6 +5

FS-32068 First Grade Math Review

Bowling Time

Follow the arrows. Add.

A. 5 → 6 → 2 = 13

A. 5 → 5 → 4 =

B. 7 → 8 → 2 =

B. 9 → 1 → 7 =

C. 2 → 7 → 3 =

C. 6 → 4 → 5 =

D. 7 → 6 → 2 =

D. 4 → 3 → 6 =

E. 8 → 1 → 3 =

E. 5 → 2 → 7 =

F. 9 → 5 → 4 =

F. 7 → 3 → 4 =

G. 1 → 8 → 3 =

G. 9 → 3 → 6 =

 FS-32068 First Grade Math Review

Name_____

On the Farm

Add.

A.

3	4	6	8	1	2	6
4	1	2	3	0	7	2
+5	+7	+7	+5	+9	+4	+5
12						

B.

6	8	7	0	6	3	3
9	5	6	5	6	3	7
+2	+3	+1	+9	+6	+5	+8

C.

8	3	6	2	5	4	5
2	7	8	5	1	4	8
+6	+5	+4	+3	+8	+4	+4

D.

2	3	5	3	2	5	5
7	6	2	3	4	4	2
1	0	1	3	6	3	6
+8	+9	+6	+3	+2	+6	+5

Under the Big Top

Subtract.

A.
$$11 - 3 = 8$$
$$12 - 4$$
$$13 - 6$$
$$11 - 2$$
$$15 - 9$$
$$14 - 5$$
$$10 - 5$$

B.
$$12 - 5$$
$$14 - 7$$
$$11 - 8$$
$$13 - 4$$
$$15 - 6$$
$$11 - 9$$
$$13 - 4$$

C.
$$11 - 7$$
$$12 - 3$$
$$13 - 5$$
$$14 - 9$$
$$15 - 8$$
$$15 - 9$$
$$12 - 3$$

D.
$$14 - 8$$
$$11 - 6$$
$$12 - 9$$
$$15 - 7$$
$$11 - 4$$
$$10 - 7$$
$$11 - 7$$

E.
$$12 - 6$$
$$13 - 7$$
$$12 - 8$$
$$13 - 9$$

F.
$$11 - 5$$
$$12 - 7$$
$$13 - 8$$
$$14 - 6$$

Ace!

Subtract.

A. $11 - 2 = \underline{9}$ $12 - 9 = \underline{}$

B. $11 - 5 = \underline{}$ $13 - 4 = \underline{}$

C. $12 - 8 = \underline{}$ $12 - 4 = \underline{}$

D. $11 - 7 = \underline{}$ $12 - 5 = \underline{}$

E. $13 - 8 = \underline{}$ $15 - 8 = \underline{}$

F. $14 - 9 = \underline{}$ $11 - 6 = \underline{}$

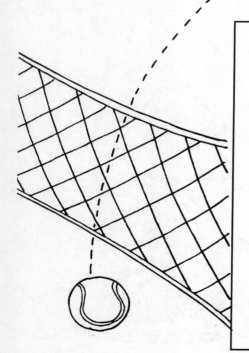

G. $11 - 3 = \underline{}$ $11 - 8 = \underline{}$

H. $14 - 7 = \underline{}$ $12 - 7 = \underline{}$

I. $13 - 7 = \underline{}$ $14 - 6 = \underline{}$

J. $15 - 9 = \underline{}$ $15 - 7 = \underline{}$

K. $13 - 6 = \underline{}$ $12 - 3 = \underline{}$

74

Reach Your Peak

Subtract.

A. 16   10   11   12   14
       − 7 − 6 − 7 − 4 − 6
        9

B. 11   13   16   11   12
       − 2 − 7 − 6 − 5 − 7

C. 11   15   13   16   14   10   10
       − 9 − 9 − 4 − 8 − 9 − 7 − 5

D. 14   17   12   11   17   15   12
       − 8 − 7 − 8 − 4 − 7 − 5 − 3

E. 14   18   14   13   11   12   13
       − 5 − 9 − 4 − 9 − 8 − 6 − 5

F. 13 − 8 = _____   17 − 9 = _____   11 − 6 = _____

G. 12 − 5 = _____   13 − 3 = _____   12 − 9 = _____

H. 15 − 7 = _____   15 − 6 = _____   14 − 7 = _____

FS-32068 First Grade Math Review

Name _____

Make the Goal

Subtract.

A. $12 - 5 =$ ___7___ $12 - 3 =$ _____ $11 - 7 =$ _____

B. $11 - 8 =$ _____ $14 - 7 =$ _____ $12 - 8 =$ _____

C. $11 - 5 =$ _____ $13 - 7 =$ _____ $16 - 9 =$ _____

D.
$$\begin{array}{r} 11 \\ -\ 3 \\ \hline \end{array} \quad \begin{array}{r} 12 \\ -\ 9 \\ \hline \end{array} \quad \begin{array}{r} 14 \\ -\ 9 \\ \hline \end{array} \quad \begin{array}{r} 14 \\ -\ 5 \\ \hline \end{array} \quad \begin{array}{r} 11 \\ -\ 9 \\ \hline \end{array} \quad \begin{array}{r} 17 \\ -\ 7 \\ \hline \end{array} \quad \begin{array}{r} 10 \\ -\ 4 \\ \hline \end{array}$$

E.
$$\begin{array}{r} 15 \\ -\ 9 \\ \hline \end{array} \quad \begin{array}{r} 13 \\ -\ 5 \\ \hline \end{array} \quad \begin{array}{r} 12 \\ -\ 4 \\ \hline \end{array} \quad \begin{array}{r} 14 \\ -\ 8 \\ \hline \end{array} \quad \begin{array}{r} 16 \\ -\ 7 \\ \hline \end{array} \quad \begin{array}{r} 12 \\ -\ 6 \\ \hline \end{array} \quad \begin{array}{r} 14 \\ -\ 4 \\ \hline \end{array}$$

F.
$$\begin{array}{r} 13 \\ -\ 4 \\ \hline \end{array} \quad \begin{array}{r} 12 \\ -\ 7 \\ \hline \end{array} \quad \begin{array}{r} 17 \\ -\ 8 \\ \hline \end{array} \quad \begin{array}{r} 11 \\ -\ 2 \\ \hline \end{array} \quad \begin{array}{r} 13 \\ -\ 6 \\ \hline \end{array} \quad \begin{array}{r} 16 \\ -\ 6 \\ \hline \end{array} \quad \begin{array}{r} 10 \\ -\ 6 \\ \hline \end{array}$$

G.
$$\begin{array}{r} 18 \\ -\ 9 \\ \hline \end{array} \quad \begin{array}{r} 16 \\ -\ 8 \\ \hline \end{array} \quad \begin{array}{r} 15 \\ -\ 6 \\ \hline \end{array} \quad \begin{array}{r} 13 \\ -\ 8 \\ \hline \end{array}$$

H.
$$\begin{array}{r} 17 \\ -\ 9 \\ \hline \end{array} \quad \begin{array}{r} 15 \\ -\ 7 \\ \hline \end{array} \quad \begin{array}{r} 15 \\ -\ 8 \\ \hline \end{array} \quad \begin{array}{r} 13 \\ -\ 9 \\ \hline \end{array}$$

FS-32068 First Grade Math Review

Secret Word

Subtract.
Color the boxes with the differences of 7 or greater yellow.
Color the boxes with the differences of 6 or less blue.

A. 18 − 9	14 − 8	17 − 9	15 − 9	13 − 4
B. 15 − 8	13 − 9	16 − 9	14 − 9	12 − 3
C. 14 − 5	17 − 8	15 − 7	13 − 8	11 − 4
D. 16 − 8	13 − 7	14 − 6	11 − 9	13 − 6
E. 15 − 6	12 − 8	16 − 7	12 − 6	11 − 3
F. 14 − 7	12 − 7	13 − 5	11 − 7	11 − 2

G. What is the secret word? _____

FS-32068 First Grade Math Review

Name_____

Three in a Row

Subtract.
Color three boxes in a row that have the same differences.

A.

13 - 8 5	11 - 6	14 - 9
13 - 5	13 - 6	15 - 5
12 - 5	11 - 8	14 - 5

B.

11 - 9	14 - 6	18 - 9
13 - 7	15 - 6	12 - 3
14 - 4	16 - 8	17 - 8

C.

10 - 7	16 - 9	13 - 6
12 - 4	17 - 9	15 - 7
16 - 6	14 - 8	11 - 5

D.

15 - 8	10 - 4	16 - 7
14 - 7	12 - 6	17 - 7
11 - 7	15 - 9	13 - 9

FS-32068 First Grade Math Review

Name _____

Pennies and nickels

Counting Money

Count each group of coins. Write the amount.

A.    6 _____ ¢

B.    _____ ¢

C.    _____ ¢

D.    _____ ¢

E.    _____ ¢

F.    _____ ¢

G.     _____ ¢

H.    _____ ¢

© Frank Schaffer Publications, Inc.

FS-32068 First Grade Math Review

Piggy Bank

Count each group of coins. Write the amount.

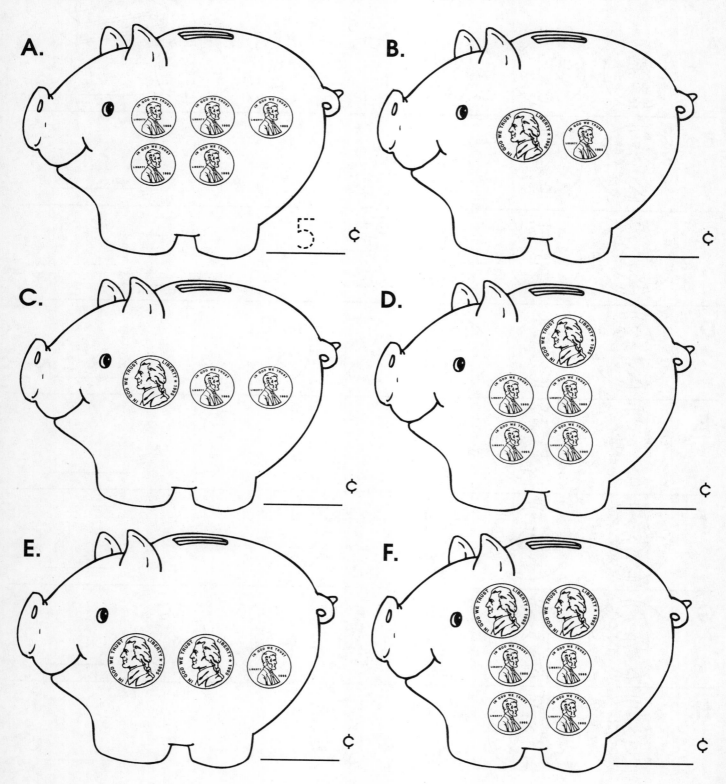

A. _5_ ¢

B. ____ ¢

C. ____ ¢

D. ____ ¢

E. ____ ¢

F. ____ ¢

FS-32068 First Grade Math Review

What's the Amount?

Count each group of coins. Write the amount.

A.

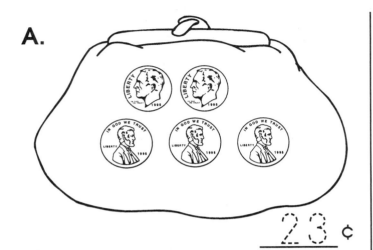

2 3 ¢

B.

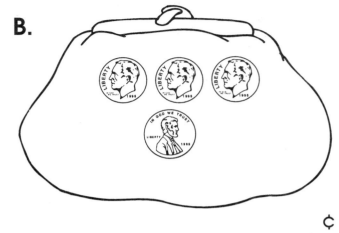

_____ ¢

C.

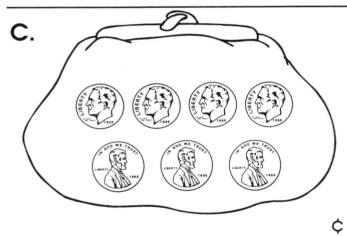

_____ ¢

D.

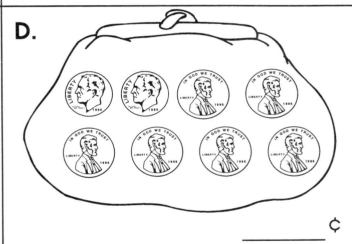

_____ ¢

E.

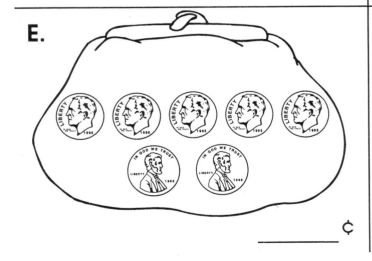

_____ ¢

F.

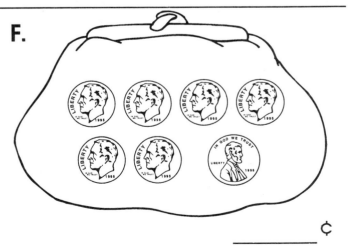

_____ ¢

What's the Price?

Count the coins in each group. Write the amount.

A.

B.

C.

D.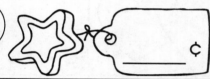

E.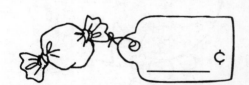

F.

G.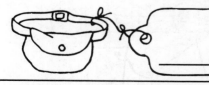

H.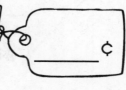

Pennies and dimes

Name

© Frank Schaffer Publications, Inc.

FS-32068 First Grade Math Review

Sticker Sale

Color the coins you need to buy each sticker.

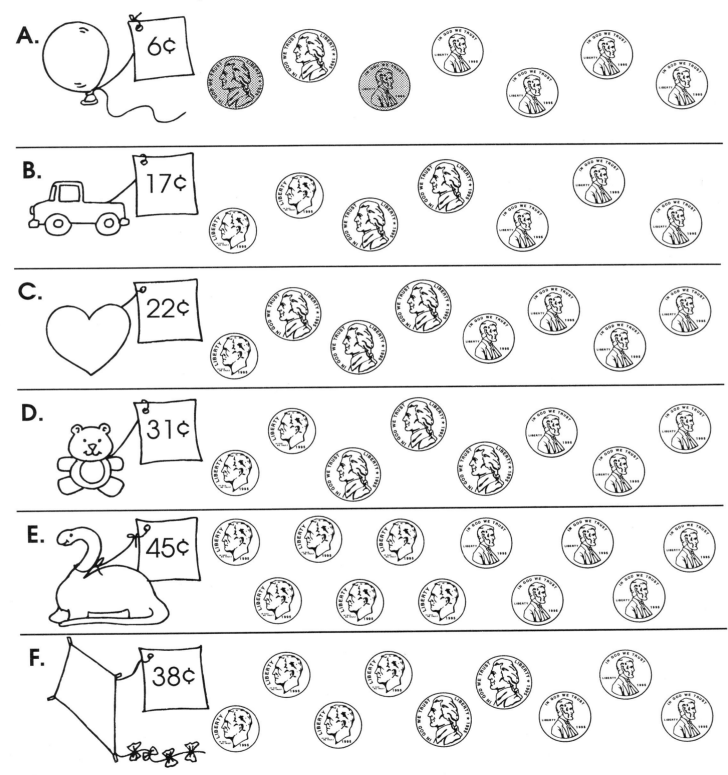

A. 6¢

B. 17¢

C. 22¢

D. 31¢

E. 45¢

F. 38¢

Name_____

Change Box

Count each group of coins. Write the amount.

A.

_37_ ¢   _____ ¢

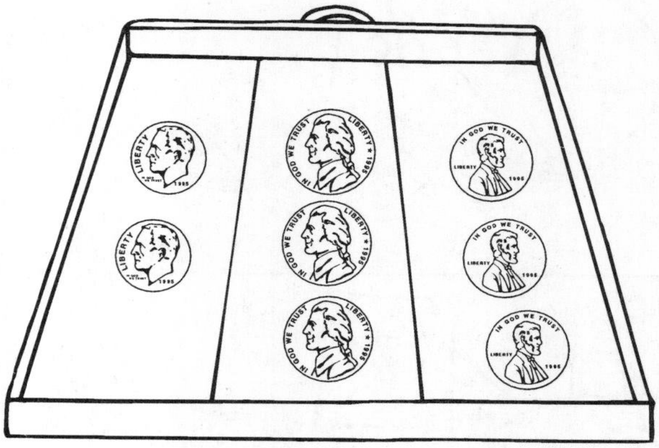

B.

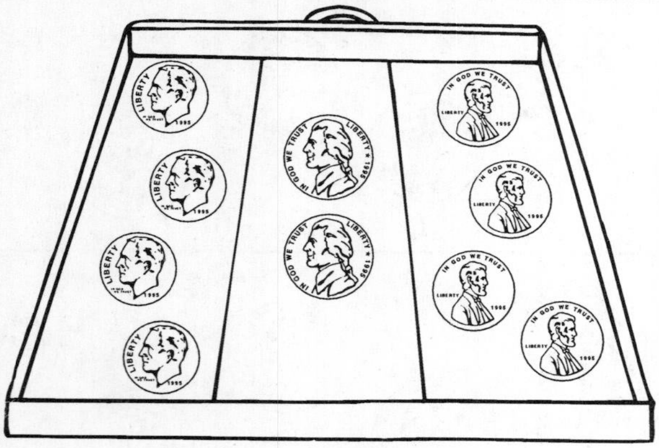

_____ ¢   _____ ¢

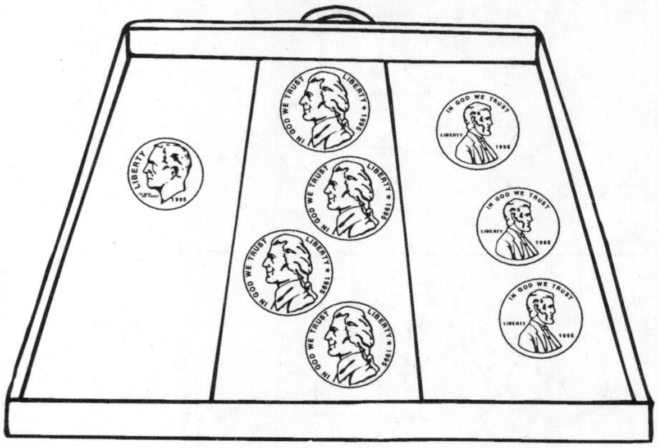

C.

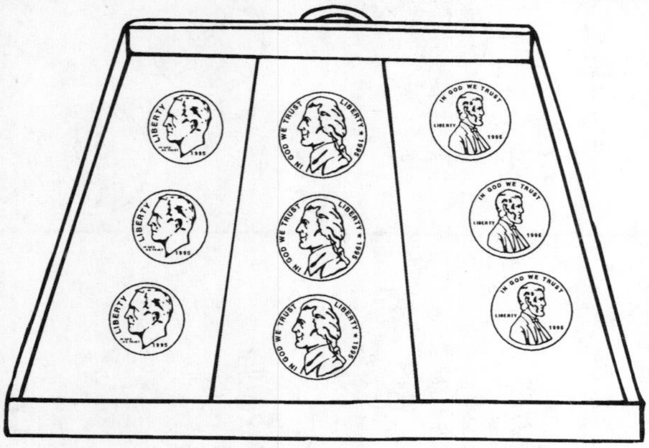

_____ ¢   _____ ¢

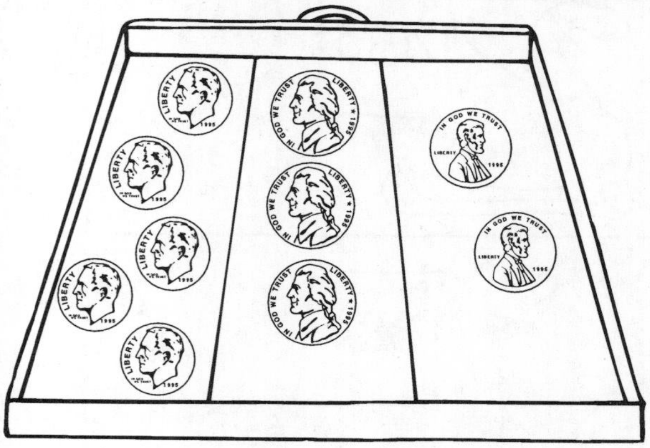

FS-32068 First Grade Math Review

Money Match

Match each group of coins to the correct amount.

A.

33¢

B.

38¢

C.

29¢

D.

41¢

E.

51¢

F.

65¢

G.

57¢

H.

75¢

FS-32068 First Grade Math Review

Shopping Spree

Cross out (X) the coins you need to buy each item.

A.

 33¢

B.

 50¢

C.

  41¢

D.

 27¢

E.

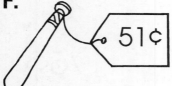 36¢

F.

51¢

FS-32068 First Grade Math Review

Telling Time

Write the time.

A.

1:00

B.

C.

FS-32068 First Grade Math Review

Show the Time

Draw the hands on each clock to show the time.

A.

5:00

3:00

7:00

B.

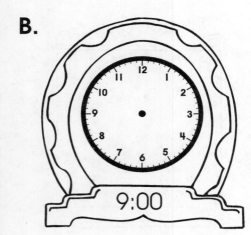
9:00

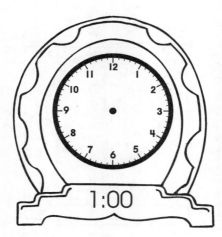
1:00

6:00

C.

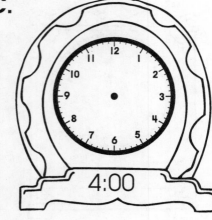
4:00

2:00

12:00

FS-32068 First Grade Math Review

What Time Is It?

Circle the correct time.

A.

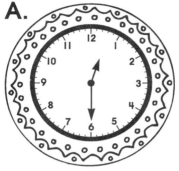   

<12:30> 1:30   2:30 3:30   5:30 6:30   10:30 11:30

B.

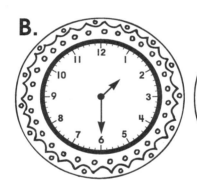  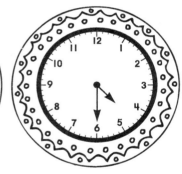 

1:30 2:30   12:30 11:30   5:30 4:30   4:30 3:30

C.

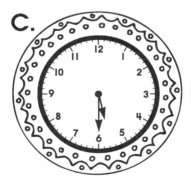   

5:30 6:30   9:30 8:30   8:30 7:30   10:30 9:30

89

What's the Time?

Draw a line from each clock to the matching time.

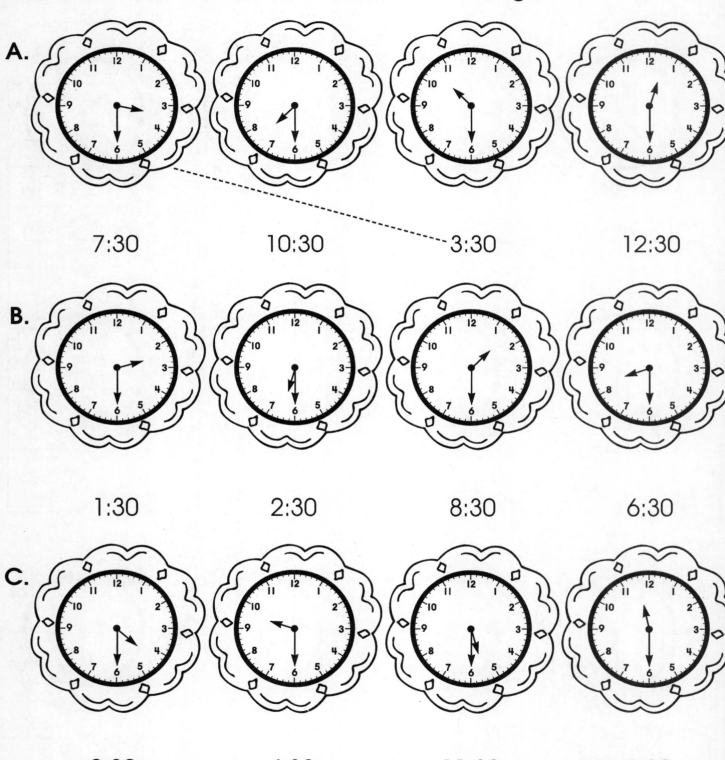

A.

7:30   10:30   3:30   12:30

B.

1:30   2:30   8:30   6:30

C.

9:30   4:30   11:30   5:30

It's a Date!

This month has 30 days.
It begins on Wednesday.
Write the dates.

Sunday	Monday	Tuesday	Wednesday	Thursday	Friday	Saturday
			¦			
		Election Day				
				Thanksgiving		

November

Answer the questions.

A. What date is Election Day? _____

B. How many Wednesdays are in November? _____

C. What date is Thanksgiving? _____

D. How many Sundays are there in this month? _____

E. What day of the week is November 13? _____

F. What day of the week is November 30? _____

The Calendar

This month has 31 days.
It begins on Monday.
Write the days.

	May					
Sunday	Monday	Tuesday	Wednesday	Thursday	Friday	Saturday
	I					

Answer the questions.

A. What date is the third Wednesday in May? _____

B. How many Sundays are in this month? _____

C. What date is between May 8 and May 10? _____

D. What day of the week is the fifth? _____

E. Starting on the 19th, how many days until the end of the month? _____

Equal Parts

Write the number of equal parts.

A.

_2_ equal parts

B.

____ equal parts

C.

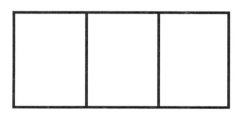

____ equal parts

D.

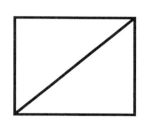

____ equal parts

E.

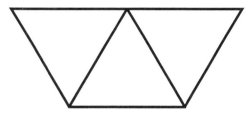

____ equal parts

F.

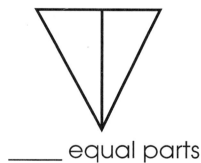

____ equal parts

G.

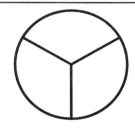

____ equal parts

H.

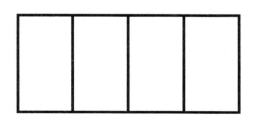

____ equal parts

FS-32068 First Grade Math Review

Equal Parts Fun

A. Color the shapes that have two equal parts.

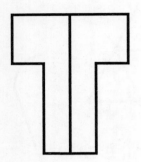 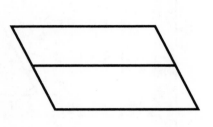 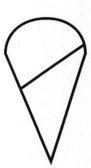 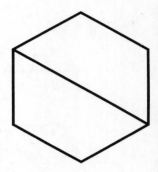

B. Color the shapes that have three equal parts.

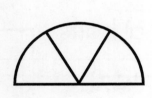 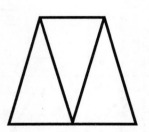 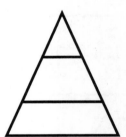 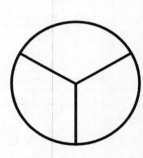

C. Color the shapes that have four equal parts.

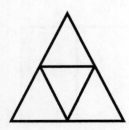 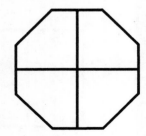 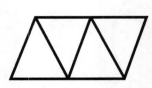 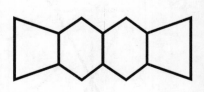

FS-32068 First Grade Math Review

Coloring Fractions

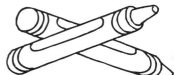

A. Color $\frac{1}{2}$.

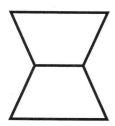  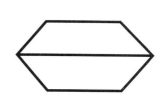 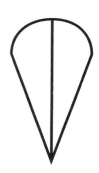

B. Color $\frac{1}{3}$.

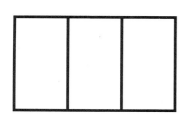 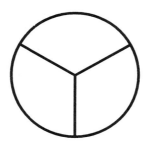 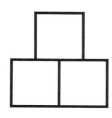 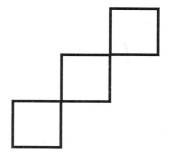

C. Color $\frac{1}{4}$.

 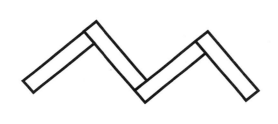 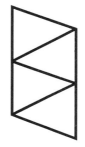 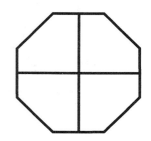

FS-32068 First Grade Math Review

Finding Fractions

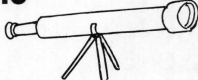

A. Color $\frac{1}{2}$ if it has equal parts.

 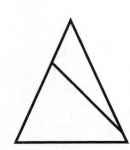 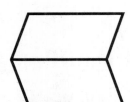 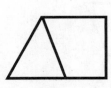 

B. Color $\frac{1}{3}$ if it has equal parts.

 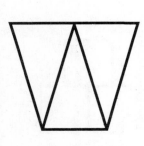 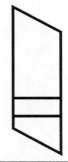 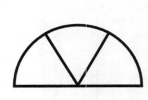 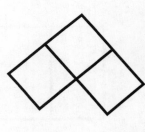

C. Color $\frac{1}{4}$ if it has equal parts.

 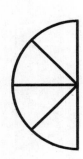 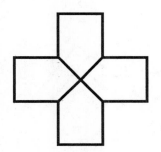 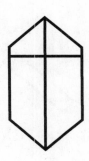 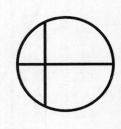

FS-32068 First Grade Math Review

Fractions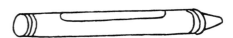

A. Color $\frac{1}{2}$ blue.

Color $\frac{1}{2}$ red.

B. Color $\frac{1}{3}$ green.

Color $\frac{1}{3}$ yellow.

Color $\frac{1}{3}$ orange.

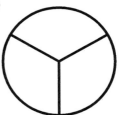

C. Color $\frac{1}{4}$ purple.

Color $\frac{1}{4}$ red.

Color $\frac{2}{4}$ green.

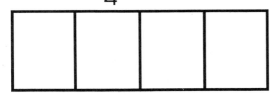

D. Color $\frac{2}{3}$ blue.

Color $\frac{1}{3}$ green.

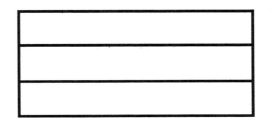

E. Color $\frac{1}{4}$ yellow.

Color $\frac{3}{4}$ red.

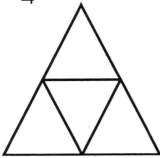

F. Color $\frac{3}{4}$ blue.

Color $\frac{1}{4}$ orange.

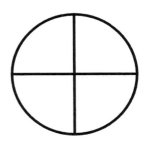

Fraction Match

Draw lines to match.

A.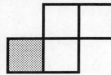

B.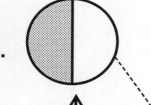

C.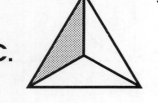

D.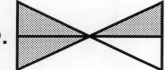

E.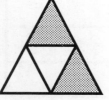

F.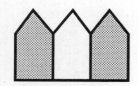

$\dfrac{1}{3}$

$\dfrac{2}{4}$

$\dfrac{3}{4}$

$\dfrac{1}{2}$

$\dfrac{2}{3}$

$\dfrac{1}{4}$

G.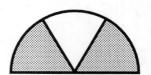

H.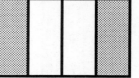

I.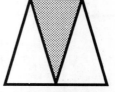

J.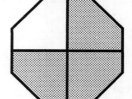

K.

L.

$\dfrac{1}{4}$

$\dfrac{1}{3}$

$\dfrac{2}{3}$

$\dfrac{3}{4}$

$\dfrac{1}{2}$

$\dfrac{2}{4}$

M. Color $\dfrac{2}{3}$.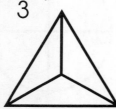

N. Color $\dfrac{2}{4}$.

FS-32068 First Grade Math Review

Name_____

Dinosaur Sums

Add.

A.

tens	ones
2	3
+ 1	4
3	7

tens	ones
1	8
+ 2	1

tens	ones
2	5
+ 2	2

B.

tens	ones
5	3
+ 1	5

tens	ones
4	0
+ 2	7

tens	ones
3	8
+ 3	1

tens	ones
1	5
+ 6	3

C.

tens	ones
8	1
+ 1	2

tens	ones
2	6
+ 5	2

tens	ones
3	7
+ 2	2

tens	ones
1	9
+ 7	0

D.

tens	ones
6	3
+ 3	6

tens	ones
2	4
+ 3	5

tens	ones
4	3
+ 5	6

tens	ones
6	0
+ 2	3

A Garden of Problems

Add.

A.

tens	ones
2	5
+ 1	3
3	8

tens	ones
4	2
+ 2	3

tens	ones
4	7
+ 3	1

tens	ones
3	6
+ 4	3

B.

tens	ones
3	5
+ 2	4

tens	ones
5	2
+ 4	2

tens	ones
3	2
+ 2	6

tens	ones
2	6
+ 5	3

C.

tens	ones
1	5
+ 7	0

tens	ones
2	7
+ 4	2

tens	ones
4	4
+ 5	5

tens	ones
7	4
+ 1	2

D.

tens	ones
5	1
+ 1	0

tens	ones
7	0
+ 2	1

tens	ones
6	5
+ 2	3

tens	ones
8	1
+ 1	8

Sailing Through Subtraction

Subtract.

A.

tens	ones
4	7
− 2	3
2	4

tens	ones
5	6
− 2	3

tens	ones
6	7
− 3	6

tens	ones
3	9
− 1	4

B.

tens	ones
5	9
− 4	1

tens	ones
4	8
− 1	5

tens	ones
2	5
− 2	0

tens	ones
6	4
− 5	1

C.

tens	ones
8	3
− 7	3

tens	ones
9	5
− 6	2

tens	ones
7	6
− 5	3

tens	ones
3	2
− 1	1

D.

tens	ones
9	8
− 3	4

tens	ones
8	7
− 2	6

tens	ones
4	9
− 3	5

FS-32068 First Grade Math Review

Bear Problems

Subtract.

A.

tens	ones
3	5
− 1	3
2	2

tens	ones
4	7
− 3	6

tens	ones
5	6
− 1	5

B.

tens	ones
2	3
− 1	3

tens	ones
7	5
− 4	2

tens	ones
8	1
− 7	0

tens	ones
9	5
− 3	4

C.

tens	ones
8	6
− 4	3

tens	ones
7	9
− 6	8

tens	ones
5	8
− 4	8

tens	ones
4	5
− 2	0

D.

tens	ones
3	3
− 1	2

tens	ones
2	8
− 1	4

tens	ones
1	7
− 1	0

tens	ones
9	9
− 5	3

Name _____

What a Ride!

Add.

A.
23	59	21	51	53	14	80
+16	+20	+37	+26	+46	+63	+19
39						

B.
15	53	24	33	82	12	62
+24	+23	+60	+41	+17	+45	+21

C.
21	33	61	85	46	72	18
+27	+52	+23	+12	+31	+17	+71

Subtract.

D.
48	83	78	49	62	68	78
−21	−31	−16	−18	−32	−21	−44
27						

E.
79	73	97	78	57	68	94
−26	−22	−34	−62	−12	−36	−52

Name _____

Champions

Add.

A.	32 + 56 88	86 + 12	83 + 14	42 + 15	64 + 21	26 + 33	13 + 66

B.	36 + 52	54 + 23	41 + 53	72 + 20	37 + 51	15 + 32	80 + 16

C.	19 + 30	76 + 22	54 + 34	62 + 25	18 + 71	24 + 32	13 + 36

Subtract.

D.	98 − 43 55	79 − 25	57 − 21	39 − 13	89 − 29	85 − 41	35 − 24

E.	49 − 32	59 − 41	73 − 21	66 − 23

F.	83 − 51	27 − 15	39 − 18	46 − 32

FS-32068 First Grade Math Review

Answer Key

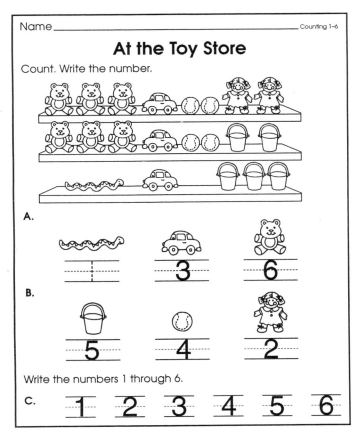

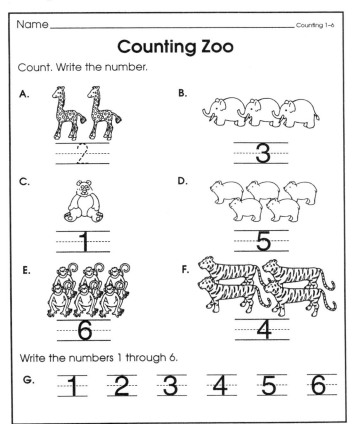

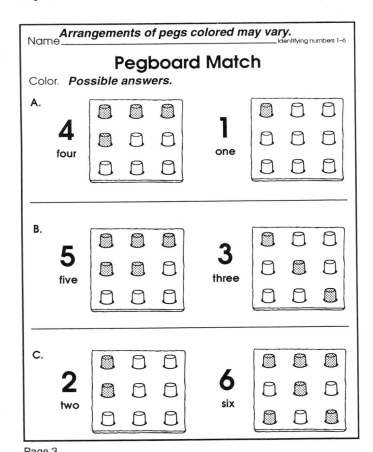

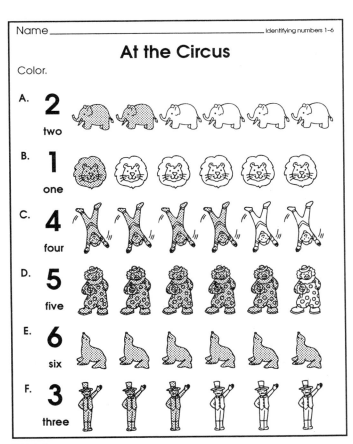

Answer Key

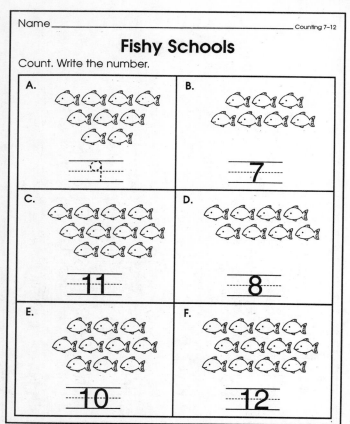

Counting 7–12

Fishy Schools

Count. Write the number.

A. _____ 4

B. _____ 7

C. _____ 11

D. _____ 8

E. _____ 10

F. _____ 12

Page 5

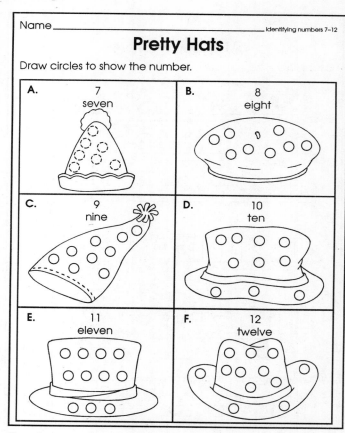

Name _____

Identifying numbers 7–12

Pretty Hats

Draw circles to show the number.

A. 7 seven

B. 8 eight

C. 9 nine

D. 10 ten

E. 11 eleven

F. 12 twelve

Page 6

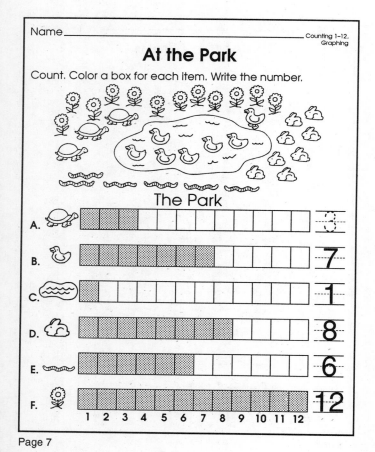

Name _____

Counting 1–12, Graphing

At the Park

Count. Color a box for each item. Write the number.

The Park

A. 3

B. 7

C. 1

D. 8

E. 6

F. 12

1 2 3 4 5 6 7 8 9 10 11 12

Page 7

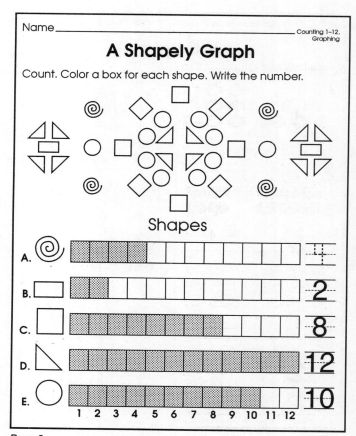

Name _____

Counting 1–12, Graphing

A Shapely Graph

Count. Color a box for each shape. Write the number.

Shapes

A. 4

B. 2

C. 8

D. 12

E. 10

1 2 3 4 5 6 7 8 9 10 11 12

Page 8

Answer Key

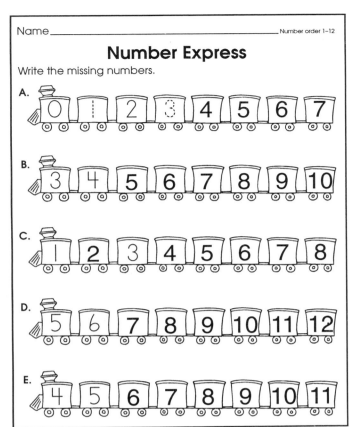

Name_____ Number order 1-12

Number Express

Write the missing numbers.

A. 0 1 2 3 4 5 6 7

B. 3 4 5 6 7 8 9 10

C. 1 2 3 4 5 6 7 8

D. 5 6 7 8 9 10 11 12

E. 4 5 6 7 8 9 10 11

Page 9

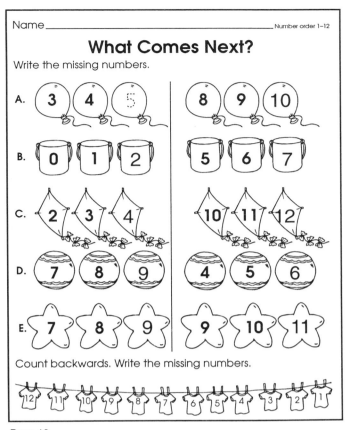

Name_____ Number order 1-12

What Comes Next?

Write the missing numbers.

A. 3 4 5   8 9 10

B. 0 1 2   5 6 7

C. 2 3 4   10 11 12

D. 7 8 9   4 5 6

E. 7 8 9   9 10 11

Count backwards. Write the missing numbers.

12 11 10 9 8 7 6 5 4 3 2 1

Page 10

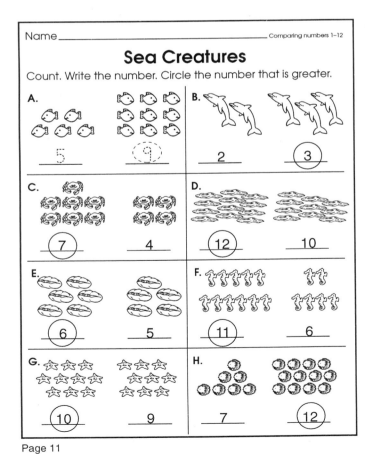

Name_____ Comparing numbers 1-12

Sea Creatures

Count. Write the number. Circle the number that is greater.

A. 5   (9)

B. 2   (3)

C. (7)   4

D. (12)   10

E. (6)   5

F. (11)   6

G. (10)   9

H. 7   (12)

Page 11

Name_____ Comparing numbers 1-12

Bear Compare

Write which number is greater and which number is less.

		greater	less			greater	less
A.	5 2	5	2	B.	4 6	6	4
C.	7 10	10	7	D.	9 8	9	8
E.	12 9	12	9	F.	11 8	11	8
G.	6 9	9	6	H.	10 11	11	10
I.	7 5	7	5	J.	12 10	12	10

Page 12

FS-32068 First Grade Math Review

Answer Key

Addition facts to 6

Adding Apples

Draw 🍎 on the trees to show the numbers.
Write how many in all.

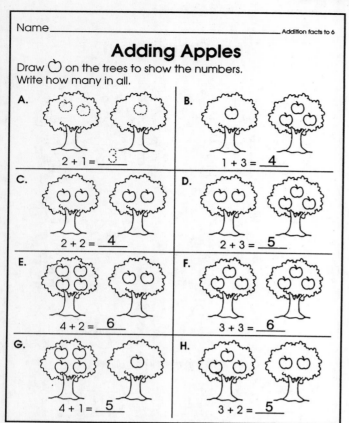

A. 2 + 1 = 3
B. 1 + 3 = 4
C. 2 + 2 = 4
D. 2 + 3 = 5
E. 4 + 2 = 6
F. 3 + 3 = 6
G. 4 + 1 = 5
H. 3 + 2 = 5

Page 13

Name_____ Addition facts to 6

Join in the Fun

Write the number sentence to go with the picture.

A. 2 + 1 = 3
B. 3 + 2 = 5
C. 2 + 2 = 4
D. 4 + 1 = 5
E. 3 + 3 = 6
F. 2 + 4 = 6
G. 5 + 1 = 6
H. 2 + 3 = 5

Page 14

Name_____ Addition facts to 6

Tune Up

Add.

A. 1 + 1 = 2   1 + 2 = 3
B. 1 + 4 = 5   2 + 3 = 5
C. 3 + 1 = 4   2 + 2 = 4   1 + 5 = 6
D. 3 + 3 = 6   5 + 1 = 6   2 + 4 = 6
E. 1 + 3 = 4   3 + 2 = 5   4 + 1 = 5
F. 3 + 1 = 4   1 + 4 = 5   2 + 3 = 5
G. 2 + 1 = 3   4 + 2 = 6   2 + 2 = 4
H. 4 + 2 = 6   3 + 3 = 6   1 + 3 = 4
I. 1 + 2 = 3   5 + 1 = 6   2 + 4 = 6
J. 1 + 5 = 6   3 + 2 = 5   3 + 1 = 4
K. 4 + 1 = 5   3 + 3 = 6   2 + 3 = 5
L. 2 + 2 = 4   2 + 4 = 6   1 + 4 = 5

Page 15

Name_____ Addition facts to 6

Rocket Ride

Add.

A.
$\begin{array}{r}1\\+1\\\hline 2\end{array}$
$\begin{array}{r}1\\+3\\\hline 4\end{array}$
$\begin{array}{r}2\\+1\\\hline 3\end{array}$
$\begin{array}{r}1\\+2\\\hline 3\end{array}$
$\begin{array}{r}1\\+3\\\hline 4\end{array}$
$\begin{array}{r}4\\+1\\\hline 5\end{array}$
$\begin{array}{r}4\\+2\\\hline 6\end{array}$

B.
$\begin{array}{r}3\\+2\\\hline 5\end{array}$
$\begin{array}{r}4\\+1\\\hline 5\end{array}$
$\begin{array}{r}5\\+1\\\hline 6\end{array}$
$\begin{array}{r}4\\+1\\\hline 5\end{array}$
$\begin{array}{r}1\\+1\\\hline 2\end{array}$
$\begin{array}{r}5\\+1\\\hline 6\end{array}$
$\begin{array}{r}2\\+1\\\hline 3\end{array}$

C.
$\begin{array}{r}1\\+4\\\hline 5\end{array}$
$\begin{array}{r}2\\+4\\\hline 6\end{array}$
$\begin{array}{r}2\\+3\\\hline 5\end{array}$
$\begin{array}{r}3\\+1\\\hline 4\end{array}$
$\begin{array}{r}5\\+1\\\hline 6\end{array}$
$\begin{array}{r}3\\+2\\\hline 5\end{array}$
$\begin{array}{r}1\\+3\\\hline 4\end{array}$

D.
$\begin{array}{r}1\\+2\\\hline 3\end{array}$
$\begin{array}{r}2\\+4\\\hline 6\end{array}$
$\begin{array}{r}4\\+2\\\hline 6\end{array}$
$\begin{array}{r}2\\+2\\\hline 4\end{array}$
$\begin{array}{r}3\\+1\\\hline 4\end{array}$
$\begin{array}{r}2\\+2\\\hline 4\end{array}$
$\begin{array}{r}1\\+5\\\hline 6\end{array}$

E.
$\begin{array}{r}1\\+5\\\hline 6\end{array}$
$\begin{array}{r}3\\+3\\\hline 6\end{array}$
$\begin{array}{r}1\\+4\\\hline 5\end{array}$
$\begin{array}{r}1\\+5\\\hline 6\end{array}$
$\begin{array}{r}2\\+2\\\hline 4\end{array}$

F.
$\begin{array}{r}3\\+2\\\hline 5\end{array}$
$\begin{array}{r}2\\+4\\\hline 6\end{array}$
$\begin{array}{r}2\\+3\\\hline 5\end{array}$
$\begin{array}{r}3\\+3\\\hline 6\end{array}$
$\begin{array}{r}1\\+1\\\hline 2\end{array}$

Page 16

108

Answer Key

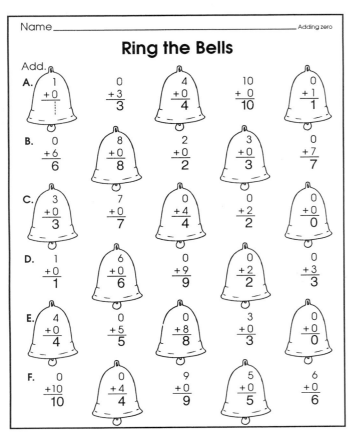

Ring the Bells

Add.

A. 1 + 0 = 1   0 + 3 = 3   4 + 0 = 4   10 + 0 = 10   0 + 1 = 1

B. 0 + 6 = 6   8 + 0 = 8   2 + 0 = 2   3 + 0 = 3   0 + 7 = 7

C. 3 + 0 = 3   7 + 0 = 7   0 + 4 = 4   0 + 2 = 2   0 + 0 = 0

D. 1 + 0 = 1   6 + 0 = 6   0 + 9 = 9   0 + 2 = 2   0 + 3 = 3

E. 4 + 0 = 4   0 + 5 = 5   0 + 8 = 8   3 + 0 = 3   0 + 0 = 0

F. 0 + 10 = 10   0 + 4 = 4   9 + 0 = 9   5 + 0 = 5   6 + 0 = 6

Page 17

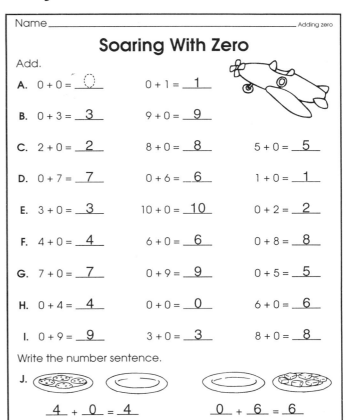

Soaring With Zero

Add.

A. 0 + 0 = 0   0 + 1 = 1

B. 0 + 3 = 3   9 + 0 = 9

C. 2 + 0 = 2   8 + 0 = 8   5 + 0 = 5

D. 0 + 7 = 7   0 + 6 = 6   1 + 0 = 1

E. 3 + 0 = 3   10 + 0 = 10   0 + 2 = 2

F. 4 + 0 = 4   6 + 0 = 6   0 + 8 = 8

G. 7 + 0 = 7   0 + 9 = 9   0 + 5 = 5

H. 0 + 4 = 4   0 + 0 = 0   6 + 0 = 6

I. 0 + 9 = 9   3 + 0 = 3   8 + 0 = 8

Write the number sentence.

J. 4 + 0 = 4   0 + 6 = 6

Page 18

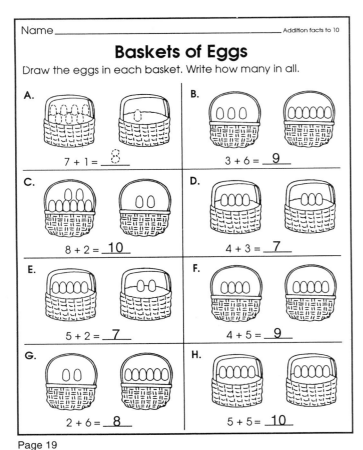

Baskets of Eggs

Draw the eggs in each basket. Write how many in all.

A. 7 + 1 = 8

B. 3 + 6 = 9

C. 8 + 2 = 10

D. 4 + 3 = 7

E. 5 + 2 = 7

F. 4 + 5 = 9

G. 2 + 6 = 8

H. 5 + 5 = 10

Page 19

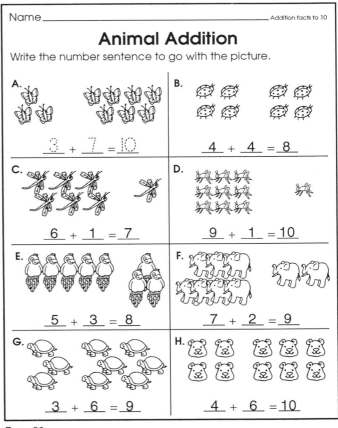

Animal Addition

Write the number sentence to go with the picture.

A. 3 + 7 = 10

B. 4 + 4 = 8

C. 6 + 1 = 7

D. 9 + 1 = 10

E. 5 + 3 = 8

F. 7 + 2 = 9

G. 3 + 6 = 9

H. 4 + 6 = 10

Page 20

Answer Key

Bubblegum Fun

Addition facts to 10

You can count on to add. Start with **5** gumballs. Count on— **five** . . . six, seven, **eight.**

5 + 3 = _8_

Count on to add.

A. 5 + 5 = _10_

B. 7 + 3 = _10_

C. 6 + 3 = _9_

D. 3 + 4 = _7_

E. 4 + 4 = _8_

F. 8 + 2 = _10_

Page 21

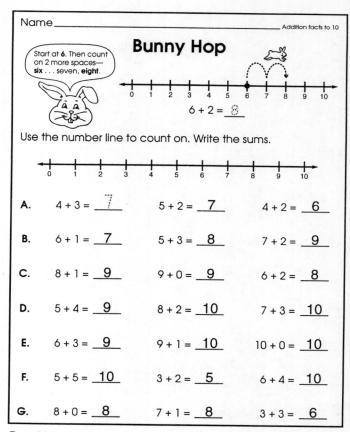

Bunny Hop

Addition facts to 10

Start at **6.** Then count on 2 more spaces— **six** . . . seven, **eight.**

6 + 2 = _8_

Use the number line to count on. Write the sums.

A. 4 + 3 = _7_   5 + 2 = _7_   4 + 2 = _6_

B. 6 + 1 = _7_   5 + 3 = _8_   7 + 2 = _9_

C. 8 + 1 = _9_   9 + 0 = _9_   6 + 2 = _8_

D. 5 + 4 = _9_   8 + 2 = _10_   7 + 3 = _10_

E. 6 + 3 = _9_   9 + 1 = _10_   10 + 0 = _10_

F. 5 + 5 = _10_   3 + 2 = _5_   6 + 4 = _10_

G. 8 + 0 = _8_   7 + 1 = _8_   3 + 3 = _6_

Page 22

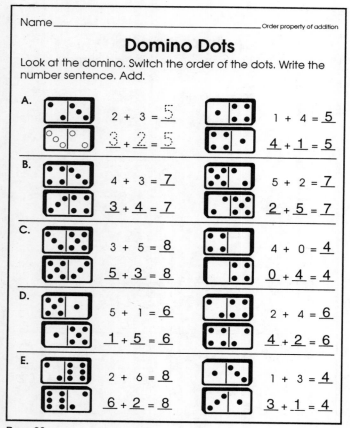

Domino Dots

Order property of addition

Look at the domino. Switch the order of the dots. Write the number sentence. Add.

A. 2 + 3 = _5_   3 + 2 = _5_   1 + 4 = _5_   4 + 1 = _5_

B. 4 + 3 = _7_   3 + 4 = _7_   5 + 2 = _7_   2 + 5 = _7_

C. 3 + 5 = _8_   5 + 3 = _8_   4 + 0 = _4_   0 + 4 = _4_

D. 5 + 1 = _6_   1 + 5 = _6_   2 + 4 = _6_   4 + 2 = _6_

E. 2 + 6 = _8_   6 + 2 = _8_   1 + 3 = _4_   3 + 1 = _4_

Page 23

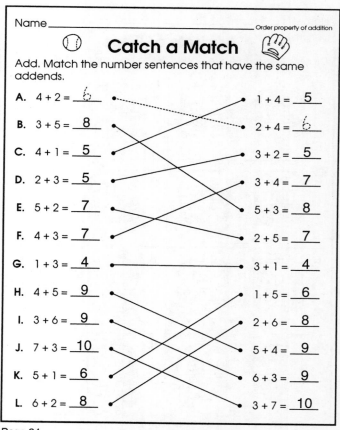

Catch a Match

Order property of addition

Add. Match the number sentences that have the same addends.

A. 4 + 2 = _6_   1 + 4 = _5_
B. 3 + 5 = _8_   2 + 4 = _6_
C. 4 + 1 = _5_   3 + 2 = _5_
D. 2 + 3 = _5_   3 + 4 = _7_
E. 5 + 2 = _7_   5 + 3 = _8_
F. 4 + 3 = _7_   2 + 5 = _7_
G. 1 + 3 = _4_   3 + 1 = _4_
H. 4 + 5 = _9_   1 + 5 = _6_
I. 3 + 6 = _9_   2 + 6 = _8_
J. 7 + 3 = _10_   5 + 4 = _9_
K. 5 + 1 = _6_   6 + 3 = _9_
L. 6 + 2 = _8_   3 + 7 = _10_

Page 24

Answer Key

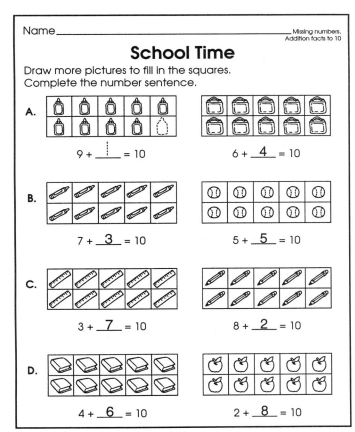

Missing numbers,
Addition facts to 10

School Time

Draw more pictures to fill in the squares.
Complete the number sentence.

A. 9 + __1__ = 10   6 + __4__ = 10

B. 7 + __3__ = 10   5 + __5__ = 10

C. 3 + __7__ = 10   8 + __2__ = 10

D. 4 + __6__ = 10   2 + __8__ = 10

Page 25

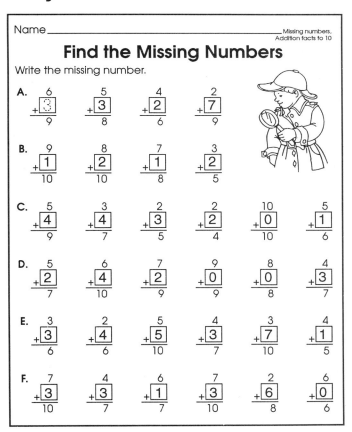

Name

Missing numbers,
Addition facts to 10

Find the Missing Numbers

Write the missing number.

A. 6+|3|=9   5+|3|=8   4+|2|=6   2+|7|=9

B. 9+|1|=10 8+|2|=10 7+|1|=8   3+|2|=5

C. 5+|4|=9   3+|4|=7   2+|3|=5   2+|2|=4   10+|0|=10 5+|1|=6

D. 5+|2|=7   6+|4|=10 7+|2|=9   9+|0|=9   8+|0|=8   4+|3|=7

E. 3+|3|=6   2+|4|=6   5+|5|=10 4+|3|=7   3+|7|=10 4+|1|=5

F. 7+|3|=10 4+|3|=7   6+|1|=7   7+|3|=10 2+|6|=8   6+|0|=6

Page 26

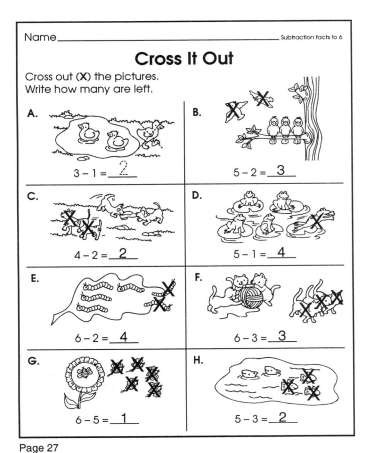

Name

Subtraction facts to 6

Cross It Out

Cross out (X) the pictures.
Write how many are left.

A. 3 − 1 = __2__   B. 5 − 2 = __3__

C. 4 − 2 = __2__   D. 5 − 1 = __4__

E. 6 − 2 = __4__   F. 6 − 3 = __3__

G. 6 − 5 = __1__   H. 5 − 3 = __2__

Page 27

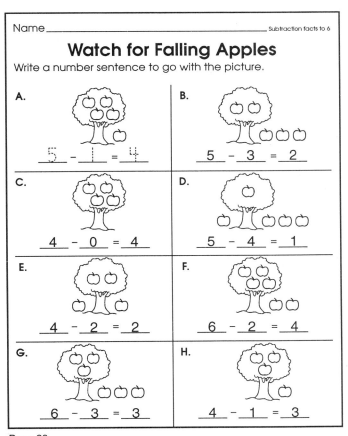

Name

Subtraction facts to 6

Watch for Falling Apples

Write a number sentence to go with the picture.

A. 5 − 1 = 4   B. 5 − 3 = 2

C. 4 − 0 = 4   D. 5 − 4 = 1

E. 4 − 2 = 2   F. 6 − 2 = 4

G. 6 − 3 = 3   H. 4 − 1 = 3

Page 28

Answer Key

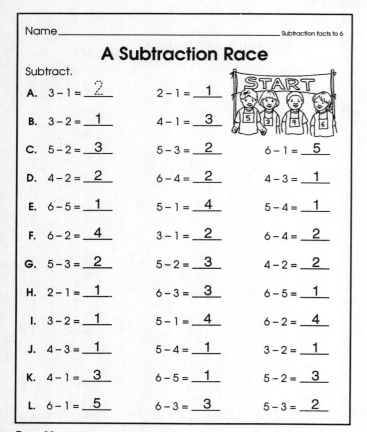

A Subtraction Race

Subtract.

Subtraction facts to 6

A.	3 – 1 = 2	2 – 1 = 1	
B.	3 – 2 = 1	4 – 1 = 3	
C.	5 – 2 = 3	5 – 3 = 2	6 – 1 = 5
D.	4 – 2 = 2	6 – 4 = 2	4 – 3 = 1
E.	6 – 5 = 1	5 – 1 = 4	5 – 4 = 1
F.	6 – 2 = 4	3 – 1 = 2	6 – 4 = 2
G.	5 – 3 = 2	5 – 2 = 3	4 – 2 = 2
H.	2 – 1 = 1	6 – 3 = 3	6 – 5 = 1
I.	3 – 2 = 1	5 – 1 = 4	6 – 2 = 4
J.	4 – 3 = 1	5 – 4 = 1	3 – 2 = 1
K.	4 – 1 = 3	6 – 5 = 1	5 – 2 = 3
L.	6 – 1 = 5	6 – 3 = 3	5 – 3 = 2

Page 29

Away We Go!

Subtract.

Subtraction facts to 6

A.	2−1=1	4−3=1	3−2=1	6−3=3	3−1=2			
B.	4−1=3	5−3=2	5−4=1	4−3=1	5−2=3	4−2=2	3−1=2	6−2=4
C.	5−1=4	6−2=4	5−2=3	3−2=1	6−1=5	6−4=2	4−3=1	5−2=3
D.	6−1=5	2−1=1	6−3=3	2−1=1	4−2=2	3−2=1	6−5=1	4−3=1
E.	3−2=1	4−1=3	5−3=2	6−3=3	6−5=1	4−2=2	6−1=5	5−4=1
F.	5−4=1	3−1=2	6−3=3	6−2=4	5−1=4	6−4=2	5−2=3	5−3=2

Page 30

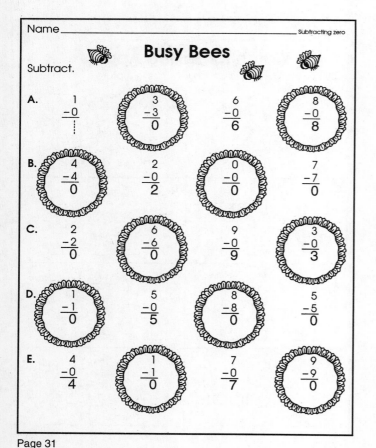

Busy Bees

Subtract.

Subtracting zero

A.	1−0=1	3−3=0	6−0=6	8−0=8
B.	4−4=0	2−0=2	0−0=0	7−7=0
C.	2−2=0	6−6=0	9−0=9	3−0=3
D.	1−1=0	5−0=5	8−8=0	5−5=0
E.	4−0=4	1−1=0	7−0=7	9−9=0

Page 31

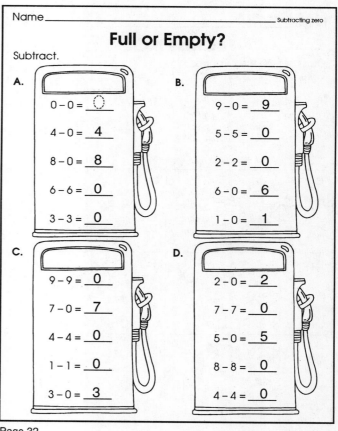

Full or Empty?

Subtract.

Subtracting zero

A.
0 – 0 = 0
4 – 0 = 4
8 – 0 = 8
6 – 6 = 0
3 – 3 = 0

B.
9 – 0 = 9
5 – 5 = 0
2 – 2 = 0
6 – 0 = 6
1 – 0 = 1

C.
9 – 9 = 0
7 – 0 = 7
4 – 4 = 0
1 – 1 = 0
3 – 0 = 3

D.
2 – 0 = 2
7 – 7 = 0
5 – 0 = 5
8 – 8 = 0
4 – 4 = 0

Page 32

FS-32068 First Grade Math Review

Answer Key

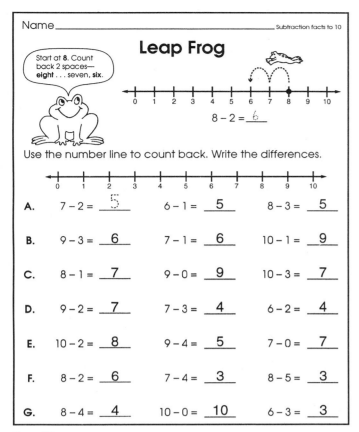

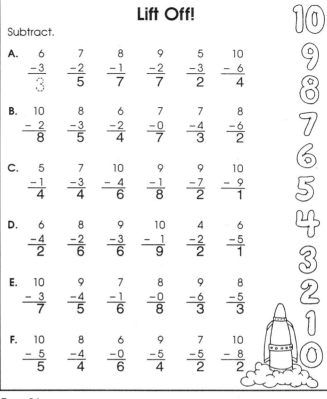

Page 33

Leap Frog

Start at **8**. Count back 2 spaces— **eight . . . seven, six.**

0 1 2 3 4 5 6 7 8 9 10

$8 - 2 = \underline{6}$

Use the number line to count back. Write the differences.

0 1 2 3 4 5 6 7 8 9 10

A. $7 - 2 = \underline{5}$ $6 - 1 = \underline{5}$ $8 - 3 = \underline{5}$

B. $9 - 3 = \underline{6}$ $7 - 1 = \underline{6}$ $10 - 1 = \underline{9}$

C. $8 - 1 = \underline{7}$ $9 - 0 = \underline{9}$ $10 - 3 = \underline{7}$

D. $9 - 2 = \underline{7}$ $7 - 3 = \underline{4}$ $6 - 2 = \underline{4}$

E. $10 - 2 = \underline{8}$ $9 - 4 = \underline{5}$ $7 - 0 = \underline{7}$

F. $8 - 2 = \underline{6}$ $7 - 4 = \underline{3}$ $8 - 5 = \underline{3}$

G. $8 - 4 = \underline{4}$ $10 - 0 = \underline{10}$ $6 - 3 = \underline{3}$

Page 33

Page 34

Lift Off!

Subtract.

A. $6 - 3 = 3$ $7 - 2 = 5$ $8 - 1 = 7$ $9 - 2 = 7$ $5 - 3 = 2$ $10 - 6 = 4$

B. $10 - 2 = 8$ $8 - 3 = 5$ $6 - 2 = 4$ $7 - 0 = 7$ $7 - 4 = 3$ $8 - 6 = 2$

C. $5 - 1 = 4$ $7 - 3 = 4$ $10 - 4 = 6$ $9 - 1 = 8$ $9 - 7 = 2$ $10 - 9 = 1$

D. $6 - 4 = 2$ $8 - 2 = 6$ $9 - 3 = 6$ $10 - 1 = 9$ $4 - 2 = 2$ $6 - 5 = 1$

E. $10 - 3 = 7$ $9 - 4 = 5$ $7 - 1 = 6$ $8 - 0 = 8$ $9 - 6 = 3$ $8 - 5 = 3$

F. $10 - 5 = 5$ $8 - 4 = 4$ $6 - 0 = 6$ $9 - 5 = 4$ $7 - 5 = 2$ $10 - 8 = 2$

Page 34

Page 35

Find the Number

Write the missing number.

A. $6 - \boxed{2} = 4$ $7 - \boxed{1} = 6$ $8 - \boxed{0} = 8$ $5 - \boxed{3} = 2$ $6 - \boxed{1} = 5$ $8 - \boxed{0} = 8$

B. $5 - \boxed{2} = 3$ $9 - \boxed{1} = 8$ $10 - \boxed{2} = 8$ $9 - \boxed{9} = 0$ $4 - \boxed{2} = 2$ $9 - \boxed{5} = 4$

C. $6 - \boxed{3} = 3$ $8 - \boxed{1} = 7$ $9 - \boxed{2} = 7$ $7 - \boxed{0} = 7$ $5 - \boxed{0} = 5$ $4 - \boxed{3} = 1$

D. $10 - \boxed{1} = 9$ $9 - \boxed{0} = 9$ $7 - \boxed{3} = 4$ $8 - \boxed{2} = 6$ $6 - \boxed{6} = 0$ $10 - \boxed{6} = 4$

E. $5 - \boxed{5} = 0$ $10 - \boxed{4} = 6$ $8 - \boxed{3} = 5$ $7 - \boxed{5} = 2$

F. $9 - \boxed{3} = 6$ $6 - \boxed{4} = 2$ $8 - \boxed{4} = 4$ $10 - \boxed{3} = 7$

Page 35

Page 36

Surprise!

Subtract.

A.

Subtract 1	
9	8
5	4
6	5
10	9
7	6

Subtract 3	
10	7
6	3
4	1
8	5
9	6

Subtract 0	
6	6
8	8
9	9
7	7
3	3

Subtract 2	
8	6
9	7
10	8
5	3
7	5

B.

Subtract 2	
10	8
7	5
8	6
6	4
9	7

Subtract 5	
5	0
7	2
6	1
9	4
10	5

Subtract 6	
10	4
6	0
7	1
9	3
8	2

Subtract 4	
10	6
7	3
8	4
6	2
9	5

C.

Subtract 7	
8	1
10	3
9	2
7	0

Subtract 1	
4	3
2	1
3	2
1	0

Subtract 2	
6	4
3	1
4	2
2	0

Page 36

Answer Key

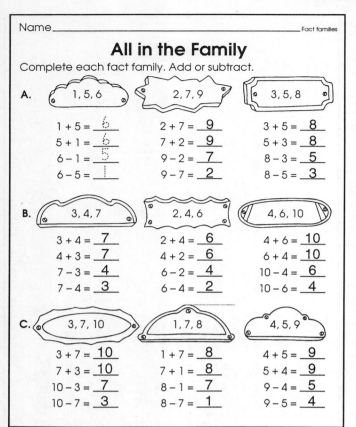

Name_____ Fact families

All in the Family

Complete each fact family. Add or subtract.

A. 1, 5, 6

$1 + 5 = 6$
$5 + 1 = 6$
$6 - 1 = 5$
$6 - 5 = 1$

2, 7, 9

$2 + 7 = 9$
$7 + 2 = 9$
$9 - 2 = 7$
$9 - 7 = 2$

3, 5, 8

$3 + 5 = 8$
$5 + 3 = 8$
$8 - 3 = 5$
$8 - 5 = 3$

B. 3, 4, 7

$3 + 4 = 7$
$4 + 3 = 7$
$7 - 3 = 4$
$7 - 4 = 3$

2, 4, 6

$2 + 4 = 6$
$4 + 2 = 6$
$6 - 2 = 4$
$6 - 4 = 2$

4, 6, 10

$4 + 6 = 10$
$6 + 4 = 10$
$10 - 4 = 6$
$10 - 6 = 4$

C. 3, 7, 10

$3 + 7 = 10$
$7 + 3 = 10$
$10 - 3 = 7$
$10 - 7 = 3$

1, 7, 8

$1 + 7 = 8$
$7 + 1 = 8$
$8 - 1 = 7$
$8 - 7 = 1$

4, 5, 9

$4 + 5 = 9$
$5 + 4 = 9$
$9 - 4 = 5$
$9 - 5 = 4$

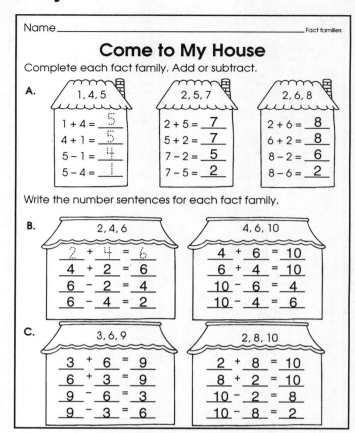

Name_____ Fact families

Come to My House

Complete each fact family. Add or subtract.

A. 1, 4, 5

$1 + 4 = 5$
$4 + 1 = 5$
$5 - 1 = 4$
$5 - 4 = 1$

2, 5, 7

$2 + 5 = 7$
$5 + 2 = 7$
$7 - 2 = 5$
$7 - 5 = 2$

2, 6, 8

$2 + 6 = 8$
$6 + 2 = 8$
$8 - 2 = 6$
$8 - 6 = 2$

Write the number sentences for each fact family.

B. 2, 4, 6

$2 + 4 = 6$
$4 + 2 = 6$
$6 - 2 = 4$
$6 - 4 = 2$

4, 6, 10

$4 + 6 = 10$
$6 + 4 = 10$
$10 - 6 = 4$
$10 - 4 = 6$

C. 3, 6, 9

$3 + 6 = 9$
$6 + 3 = 9$
$9 - 6 = 3$
$9 - 3 = 6$

2, 8, 10

$2 + 8 = 10$
$8 + 2 = 10$
$10 - 2 = 8$
$10 - 8 = 2$

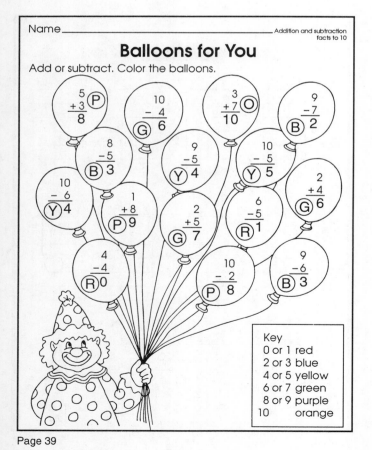

Name_____ Addition and subtraction facts to 10

Balloons for You

Add or subtract. Color the balloons.

$5 + 3 = 8$ (P)
$10 - 4 = 6$ (G)
$3 + 7 = 10$ (O)
$9 - 7 = 2$ (B)
$8 - 5 = 3$ (B)
$9 - 5 = 4$ (Y)
$10 - 5 = 5$ (Y)
$10 - 6 = 4$ (Y)
$1 + 8 = 9$ (P)
$2 + 5 = 7$ (G)
$6 - 5 = 1$ (R)
$2 + 4 = 6$ (G)
$4 - 4 = 0$ (R)
$10 - 2 = 8$ (P)
$9 - 6 = 3$ (B)

Key
0 or 1 red
2 or 3 blue
4 or 5 yellow
6 or 7 green
8 or 9 purple
10   orange

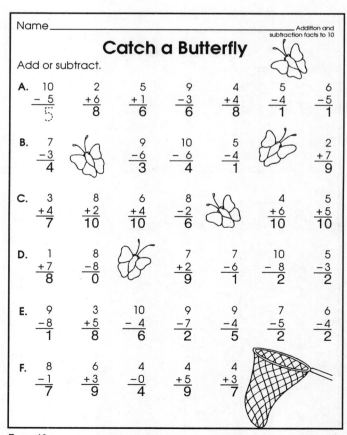

Name_____ Addition and subtraction facts to 10

Catch a Butterfly

Add or subtract.

A.
$10 - 5 = 5$
$2 + 6 = 8$
$5 + 1 = 6$
$9 - 3 = 6$
$4 + 4 = 8$
$5 - 4 = 1$
$6 - 5 = 1$

B.
$7 - 3 = 4$
$9 - 6 = 3$
$10 - 6 = 4$
$5 - 4 = 1$
$2 + 7 = 9$

C.
$3 + 4 = 7$
$8 + 2 = 10$
$6 + 4 = 10$
$8 - 2 = 6$
$4 + 6 = 10$
$5 + 5 = 10$

D.
$1 + 7 = 8$
$8 - 8 = 0$
$7 + 2 = 9$
$7 - 6 = 1$
$10 - 8 = 2$
$5 - 3 = 2$

E.
$9 - 8 = 1$
$3 + 5 = 8$
$10 - 4 = 6$
$9 - 7 = 2$
$9 - 4 = 5$
$7 - 5 = 2$
$6 - 4 = 2$

F.
$8 - 1 = 7$
$6 + 3 = 9$
$4 - 0 = 4$
$4 + 5 = 9$
$4 + 3 = 7$

114

Answer Key

Find the Solid Shape
Color each object that has the same shape.

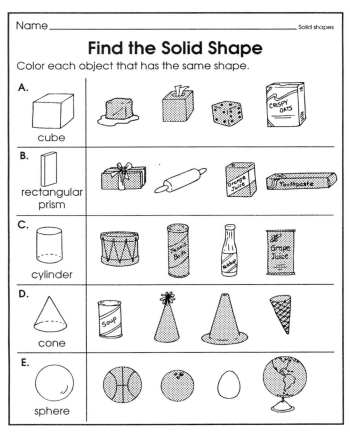

A. cube
B. rectangular prism
C. cylinder
D. cone
E. sphere

Page 41

Solids
Cross out (X) the shape that does not belong.

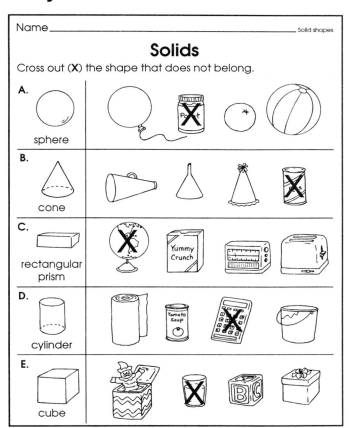

A. sphere
B. cone
C. rectangular prism
D. cylinder
E. cube

Page 42

Plane Shapes

circle · square · triangle · rectangle

Color the circles green.
Color the triangles red.
Color the rectangles blue.
Color the squares yellow.

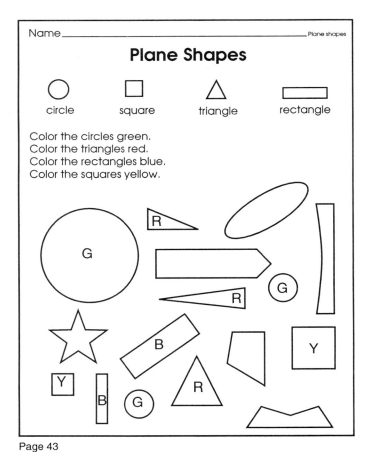

Page 43

How Many Can You Find?

circle · square · triangle · rectangle

Color the circles green.
Color the triangles red.
Color the rectangles blue.
Color the squares yellow.

Color as directed.

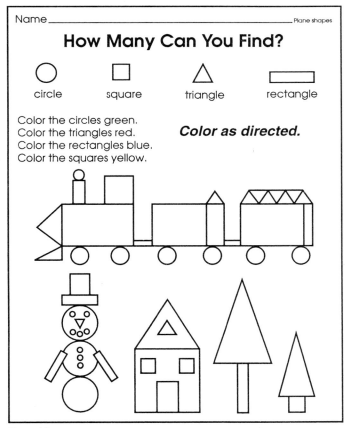

Page 44

FS-32068 First Grade Math Review

Answer Key

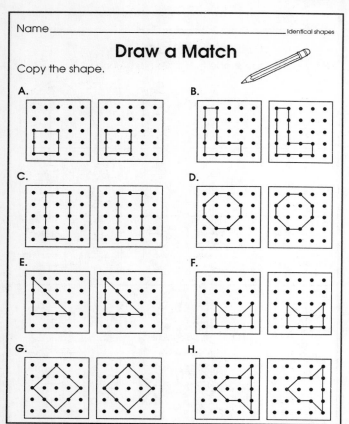

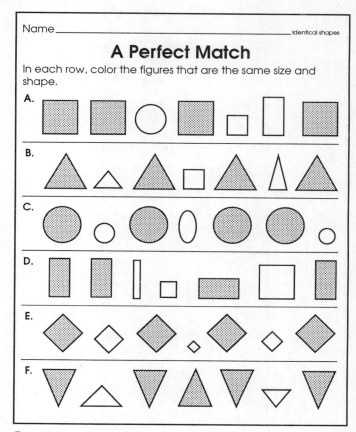

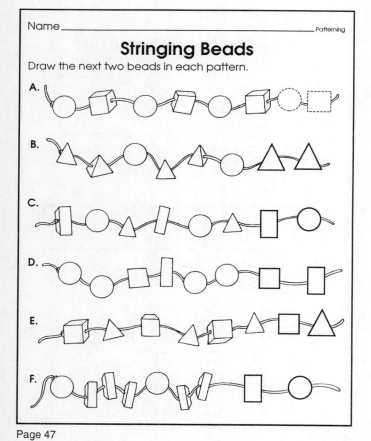

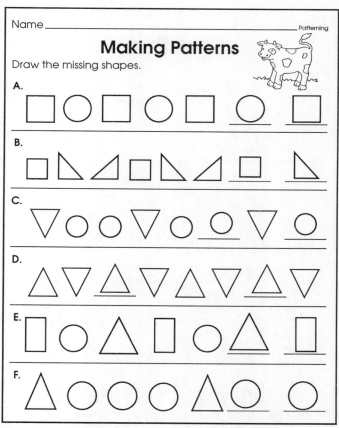

116

Answer Key

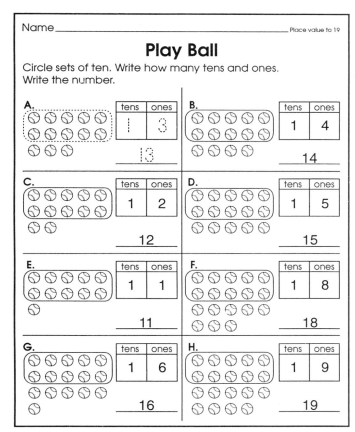

Play Ball

Circle sets of ten. Write how many tens and ones.
Write the number.

A.
tens	ones
1	3
13

B.
tens	ones
1	4
14

C.
tens	ones
1	2
12

D.
tens	ones
1	5
15

E.
tens	ones
1	1
11

F.
tens	ones
1	8
18

G.
tens	ones
1	6
16

H.
tens	ones
1	9
19

Page 49

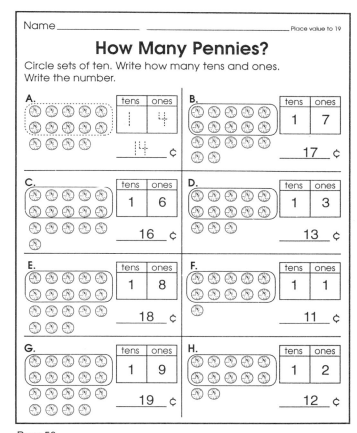

How Many Pennies?

Circle sets of ten. Write how many tens and ones.
Write the number.

A.
tens	ones
1	4
14 ¢

B.
tens	ones
1	7
17 ¢

C.
tens	ones
1	6
16 ¢

D.
tens	ones
1	3
13 ¢

E.
tens	ones
1	8
18 ¢

F.
tens	ones
1	1
11 ¢

G.
tens	ones
1	9
19 ¢

H.
tens	ones
1	2
12 ¢

Page 50

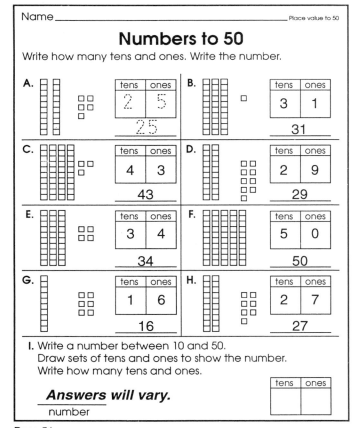

Numbers to 50

Write how many tens and ones. Write the number.

A.
tens	ones
2	5
25

B.
tens	ones
3	1
31

C.
tens	ones
4	3
43

D.
tens	ones
2	9
29

E.
tens	ones
3	4
34

F.
tens	ones
5	0
50

G.
tens	ones
1	6
16

H.
tens	ones
2	7
27

I. Write a number between 10 and 50.
Draw sets of tens and ones to show the number.
Write how many tens and ones.

Answers will vary.

tens	ones

number

Page 51

Color the Number

Color to show the number.
Write how many tens and ones.

A. Color 23
tens	ones
2	3

B. Color 42
tens	ones
4	2

C. Color 36
tens	ones
3	6

D. Color 21
tens	ones
2	1

E. Color 15
tens	ones
1	5

Page 52

Answer Key

Page 53

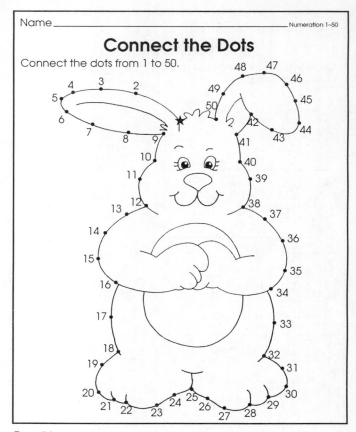

Page 54

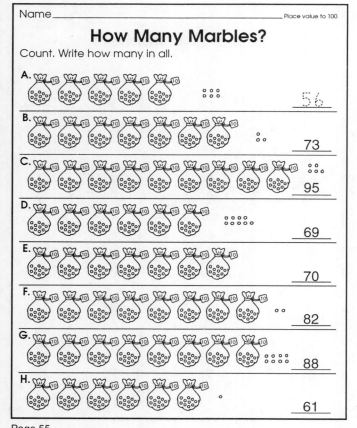

Page 55

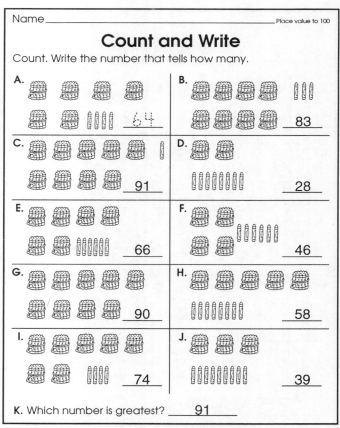

Page 56

Answer Key

An Elephant Joke

Name _____ Numeration 1–100

Write the missing numbers.

A.	25, **26**, 27 — **O**	28, 29, **30** — **E**	**31**, 32, 33 — **R**
B.	**36**, 37, 38 — **A**	39, **40**, 41 — **E**	42, 43, **44** — **I**
C.	**70**, 71, 72 — **E**	73, **74**, 75 — **S**	76, **77**, 78 — **W**
D.	62, **63**, 64 — **N**	65, 66, **67** — **H**	**47**, 48, 49 — **D**
E.	**58**, 59, 60 — **R**	61, **62**, 63 — **T**	64, **65**, 66 — **A**
F.	86, **87**, 88 — **S**	**89**, 90, 91 — **E**	92, 93, **94** — **N**

Fill in the correct letter over each answer. Why does an elephant wear green sneakers instead of red ones?

HIS R E D O N E S A R E
     31 70 47 26 94 30 74 36 58 40

I N T H E W A S H.
44 63 62 67 89 77 65 87

Page 57

What's Missing?

Name _____ Numeration 1–100

Write the missing numbers.

A.

1	2	3	4	5	6	7	8	9	10
11	12	13	14	15	16	17	18	19	20
21	22	23	24	25	26	27	28	29	30
31	32	33	34	35	36	37	38	39	40
41	42	43	44	45	46	47	48	49	50
51	52	53	54	55	56	57	58	59	60
61	62	63	64	65	66	67	68	69	70
71	72	73	74	75	76	77	78	79	80
81	82	83	84	85	86	87	88	89	90
91	92	93	94	95	96	97	98	99	100

B. Color the numbers between 43 and 47 red.

C. Color the number that comes just after 58 blue.

D. Color the number that comes just before 90 yellow.

E. Color the number between 29 and 31 orange.

F. Color the number that comes just after 99 green.

G. Color the numbers between 71 and 75 purple.

Page 58

X's and O's

Name _____ Greater than, Less than, Numeration 1–100

Look at the first number in each row.
Cross out (**X**) the numbers that are greater.
Circle the numbers that are less.

A. 43   (36)   ~~75~~   (29)   50

B. 36   ~~X~~   (26)   ~~X~~   (35)

C. 75   (74)   (57)   ~~X~~   (69)

D. 18   ~~X~~   (16)   ~~X~~   9

E. 64   (46)   (63)   ~~X~~   ~~X~~

F. 59   (45)   (58)   ~~X~~   ~~X~~

G. 80   (19)   ~~X~~   ~~X~~   (79)

H. 92   ~~X~~   (89)   (90)   ~~X~~

Page 59

Building Blocks

Name _____ Greater than, Less than, Numeration 1–100

Write two 2-digit numbers from each pair of blocks.
Circle the greater number.

A. 6   1 → 16   (61)

B. 4   8 → 48   (84)

C. 2   5 → 25   (52)

D. 5   3 → (53)   35

E. 8   6 → 86   (68)

F. 1   7 → 17   (71)

G. 9   2 → (92)   29

H. 3   4 → 34   (43)

Page 60

FS-32068 First Grade Math Review

Answer Key

Name_____   Skip-counting

Skip-Counting

A. Count by twos. Write the numbers.

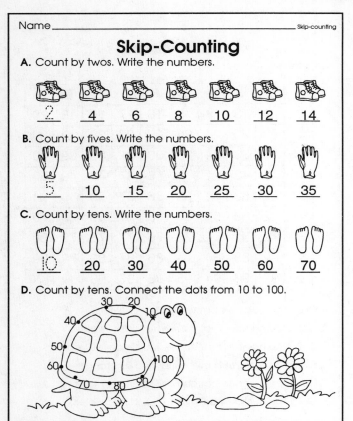

2   4   6   8   10   12   14

B. Count by fives. Write the numbers.

5   10   15   20   25   30   35

C. Count by tens. Write the numbers.

10   20   30   40   50   60   70

D. Count by tens. Connect the dots from 10 to 100.

Page 61

Name_____   Skip-counting

Climb the Ladders

Count by twos, fives, or tens. Write the missing numbers.

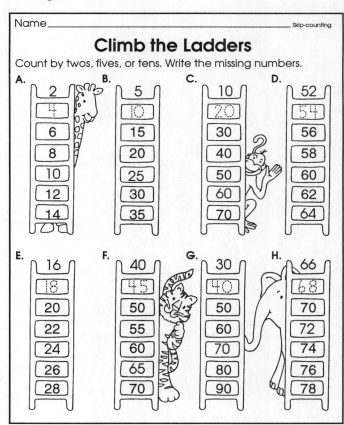

A.	B.	C.	D.
2	5	10	52
4	10	20	54
6	15	30	56
8	20	40	58
10	25	50	60
12	30	60	62
14	35	70	64

E.	F.	G.	H.
16	40	30	66
18	45	40	68
20	50	50	70
22	55	60	72
24	60	70	74
26	65	80	76
28	70	90	78

Page 62

Name_____   Doubles facts,
                                                   Addition facts to 18

Double It

Add.

A.
4	7	1	3	2
+4	+7	+1	+3	+2
8	14	2	6	4

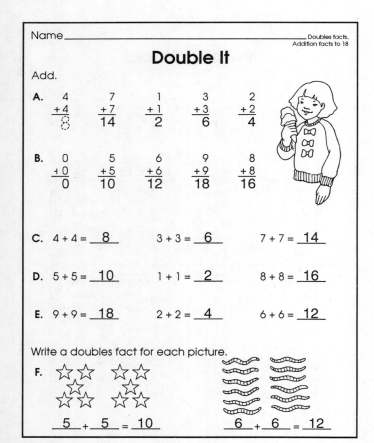

B.
0	5	6	9	8
+0	+5	+6	+9	+8
0	10	12	18	16

C. 4 + 4 = 8   3 + 3 = 6   7 + 7 = 14

D. 5 + 5 = 10   1 + 1 = 2   8 + 8 = 16

E. 9 + 9 = 18   2 + 2 = 4   6 + 6 = 12

Write a doubles fact for each picture.

F.

5 + 5 = 10   6 + 6 = 12

Page 63

Name_____   Doubles facts,
                                                   Addition facts to 18

Twice as Nice

Add.

A.
4	5	6	7	5
+4	+5	+6	+7	+5
8	10	12	14	10

B.
8	9	3	4	5
+8	+9	+3	+4	+5
16	18	6	8	10

C.
9	0	2	1	7
+9	+0	+2	+1	+7
18	0	4	2	14

Use a doubles fact to solve each riddle.

D. My double is 12.
Who am I?

6 + 6

E. My double is 10.
Who am I?

5 + 5

F. My double is 16.
Who am I?

8 + 8

G. My double is 14.
Who am I?

7 + 7

Page 64

FS-32068 First Grade Math Review

Answer Key

Addition Wheels

Add to complete the addition wheels.

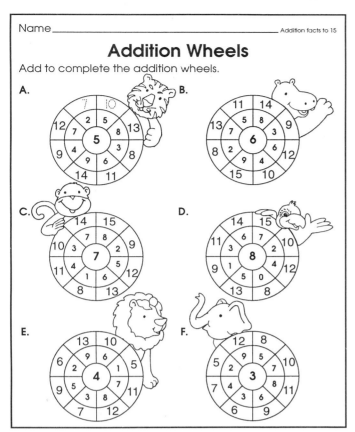

Pop the Balloons

Add.
Color the balloons that match the sum on each dart.

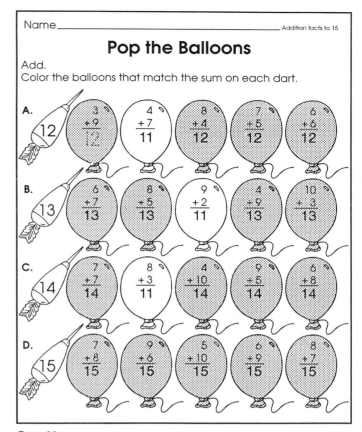

A. 12 — $\frac{3}{+9}{12}$ | $\frac{4}{+7}{11}$ | $\frac{8}{+4}{12}$ | $\frac{7}{+5}{12}$ | $\frac{6}{+6}{12}$

B. 13 — $\frac{6}{+7}{13}$ | $\frac{8}{+5}{13}$ | $\frac{9}{+2}{11}$ | $\frac{4}{+9}{13}$ | $\frac{10}{+3}{13}$

C. 14 — $\frac{7}{+7}{14}$ | $\frac{8}{+3}{11}$ | $\frac{4}{+10}{14}$ | $\frac{9}{+5}{14}$ | $\frac{6}{+8}{14}$

D. 15 — $\frac{7}{+8}{15}$ | $\frac{9}{+6}{15}$ | $\frac{5}{+10}{15}$ | $\frac{6}{+9}{15}$ | $\frac{8}{+7}{15}$

Magic Carpet Ride

Add.

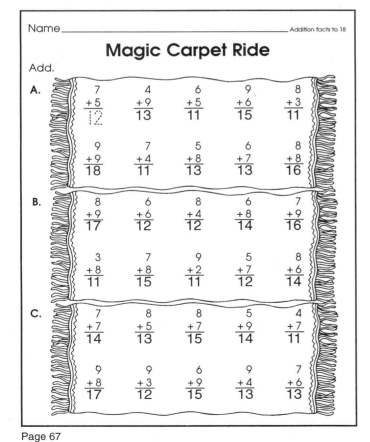

A. $\frac{7}{+5}{12}$ | $\frac{4}{+9}{13}$ | $\frac{6}{+5}{11}$ | $\frac{9}{+6}{15}$ | $\frac{8}{+3}{11}$

$\frac{9}{+9}{18}$ | $\frac{7}{+4}{11}$ | $\frac{5}{+8}{13}$ | $\frac{6}{+7}{13}$ | $\frac{8}{+8}{16}$

B. $\frac{8}{+9}{17}$ | $\frac{6}{+6}{12}$ | $\frac{8}{+4}{12}$ | $\frac{6}{+8}{14}$ | $\frac{7}{+9}{16}$

$\frac{3}{+8}{11}$ | $\frac{7}{+8}{15}$ | $\frac{9}{+2}{11}$ | $\frac{5}{+7}{12}$ | $\frac{8}{+6}{14}$

C. $\frac{7}{+7}{14}$ | $\frac{8}{+5}{13}$ | $\frac{8}{+7}{15}$ | $\frac{5}{+9}{14}$ | $\frac{4}{+7}{11}$

$\frac{9}{+8}{17}$ | $\frac{9}{+3}{12}$ | $\frac{6}{+9}{15}$ | $\frac{9}{+4}{13}$ | $\frac{7}{+6}{13}$

Double Bubble

Add.

A. 5 + 5 = 10 | 5 + 4 = 9 | 5 + 7 = 12
B. 6 + 5 = 11 | 5 + 0 = 5 | 9 + 2 = 11
C. 4 + 5 = 9 | 1 + 4 = 5 | 4 + 8 = 12
D. 4 + 3 = 7 | 7 + 7 = 14 | 5 + 6 = 11
E. 8 + 7 = 15 | 0 + 7 = 7 | 4 + 4 = 8
F. 8 + 8 = 16 | 8 + 5 = 13 | 3 + 4 = 7
G. 9 + 8 = 17 | 7 + 8 = 15 | 9 + 7 = 16
H. 7 + 9 = 16 | 9 + 9 = 18 | 10 + 4 = 14
I. 5 + 9 = 14 | 10 + 5 = 15 |
J. 9 + 6 = 15 | 7 + 5 = 12
K. 4 + 9 = 13 | 1 + 9 = 10
L. 6 + 0 = 6 | 6 + 4 = 10

121

Answer Key

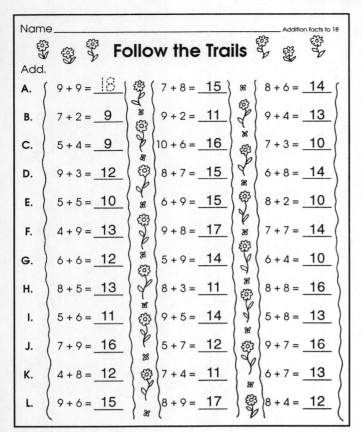

Follow the Trails

Addition facts to 18

Add.

A.	$9 + 9 = 18$	$7 + 8 = 15$	$8 + 6 = 14$
B.	$7 + 2 = 9$	$9 + 2 = 11$	$9 + 4 = 13$
C.	$5 + 4 = 9$	$10 + 6 = 16$	$7 + 3 = 10$
D.	$9 + 3 = 12$	$8 + 7 = 15$	$6 + 8 = 14$
E.	$5 + 5 = 10$	$6 + 9 = 15$	$8 + 2 = 10$
F.	$4 + 9 = 13$	$9 + 8 = 17$	$7 + 7 = 14$
G.	$6 + 6 = 12$	$5 + 9 = 14$	$6 + 4 = 10$
H.	$8 + 5 = 13$	$8 + 3 = 11$	$8 + 8 = 16$
I.	$5 + 6 = 11$	$9 + 5 = 14$	$5 + 8 = 13$
J.	$7 + 9 = 16$	$5 + 7 = 12$	$9 + 7 = 16$
K.	$4 + 8 = 12$	$7 + 4 = 11$	$6 + 7 = 13$
L.	$9 + 6 = 15$	$8 + 9 = 17$	$8 + 4 = 12$

Page 69

Valerie's Vine

Addition facts to 18

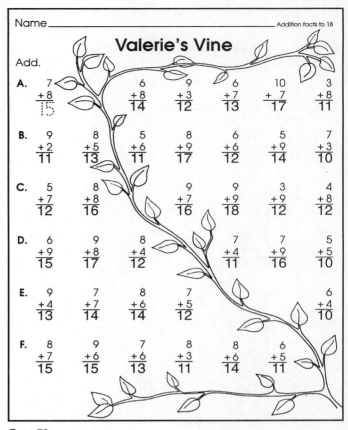

Add.

A.	7 +8 = 15	6 +8 = 14	9 +3 = 12	6 +7 = 13	10 +7 = 17	3 +8 = 11
B.	9 +2 = 11	8 +5 = 13	5 +6 = 11	8 +9 = 17	6 +6 = 12	5 +9 = 14	7 +3 = 10
C.	5 +7 = 12	8 +8 = 16	9 +7 = 16	9 +9 = 18	3 +9 = 12	4 +8 = 12
D.	6 +9 = 15	9 +8 = 17	8 +4 = 12	7 +4 = 11	7 +9 = 16	5 +5 = 10
E.	9 +4 = 13	7 +7 = 14	8 +6 = 14	7 +5 = 12	6 +4 = 10
F.	8 +7 = 15	9 +6 = 15	7 +6 = 13	8 +3 = 11	8 +6 = 14	6 +5 = 11

Page 70

Bowling Time

Three addends

Follow the arrows. Add.

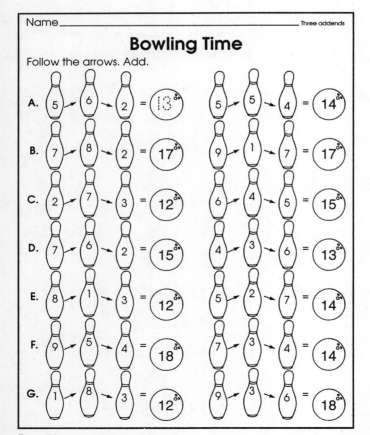

A.	5 → 6 → 2 = 13	5 → 5 → 4 = 14
B.	7 → 8 → 2 = 17	9 → 1 → 7 = 17
C.	2 → 7 → 3 = 12	6 → 4 → 5 = 15
D.	7 → 6 → 2 = 15	4 → 3 → 6 = 13
E.	8 → 1 → 3 = 12	5 → 2 → 7 = 14
F.	9 → 5 → 4 = 18	7 → 3 → 4 = 14
G.	1 → 8 → 3 = 12	9 → 3 → 6 = 18

Page 71

On the Farm

Three or four addends

Add.

A.	3 4 +5 = 12	4 1 +7 = 12	6 2 +7 = 15	8 3 +5 = 16	1 0 +9 = 10	2 7 +4 = 13	6 2 +5 = 13
B.	6 9 +2 = 17	8 5 +3 = 16	7 6 +1 = 14	0 5 +9 = 14	6 6 +6 = 18	3 3 +5 = 11	3 7 +8 = 18
C.	8 2 +6 = 16	3 7 +5 = 15	6 8 +4 = 18	2 5 +3 = 10	5 1 +8 = 14	4 4 +4 = 12	5 8 +4 = 17
D.	2 7 1 +8 = 18	3 6 0 +9 = 18	5 2 1 +6 = 14	3 3 3 +3 = 12	2 4 6 +2 = 14	5 4 3 +6 = 18	5 2 6 +5 = 18

Page 72

FS-32068 First Grade Math Review

Answer Key

Subtraction facts to 15

Under the Big Top

Subtract.

A.
| $\begin{array}{r} 11 \\ -\ 3 \\ \hline 8 \end{array}$ | $\begin{array}{r} 12 \\ -\ 4 \\ \hline 8 \end{array}$ | $\begin{array}{r} 13 \\ -\ 6 \\ \hline 7 \end{array}$ | $\begin{array}{r} 11 \\ -\ 2 \\ \hline 9 \end{array}$ | $\begin{array}{r} 15 \\ -\ 9 \\ \hline 6 \end{array}$ | $\begin{array}{r} 14 \\ -\ 5 \\ \hline 9 \end{array}$ | $\begin{array}{r} 10 \\ -\ 5 \\ \hline 5 \end{array}$ |

B.
| $\begin{array}{r} 12 \\ -\ 5 \\ \hline 7 \end{array}$ | $\begin{array}{r} 14 \\ -\ 7 \\ \hline 7 \end{array}$ | $\begin{array}{r} 11 \\ -\ 8 \\ \hline 3 \end{array}$ | $\begin{array}{r} 13 \\ -\ 4 \\ \hline 9 \end{array}$ | $\begin{array}{r} 15 \\ -\ 6 \\ \hline 9 \end{array}$ | $\begin{array}{r} 11 \\ -\ 9 \\ \hline 2 \end{array}$ | $\begin{array}{r} 13 \\ -\ 4 \\ \hline 9 \end{array}$ |

C.
| $\begin{array}{r} 11 \\ -\ 7 \\ \hline 4 \end{array}$ | $\begin{array}{r} 12 \\ -\ 3 \\ \hline 9 \end{array}$ | $\begin{array}{r} 13 \\ -\ 5 \\ \hline 8 \end{array}$ | $\begin{array}{r} 14 \\ -\ 9 \\ \hline 5 \end{array}$ | $\begin{array}{r} 15 \\ -\ 8 \\ \hline 7 \end{array}$ | $\begin{array}{r} 15 \\ -\ 9 \\ \hline 6 \end{array}$ | $\begin{array}{r} 12 \\ -\ 3 \\ \hline 9 \end{array}$ |

D.
| $\begin{array}{r} 14 \\ -\ 8 \\ \hline 6 \end{array}$ | $\begin{array}{r} 11 \\ -\ 6 \\ \hline 5 \end{array}$ | $\begin{array}{r} 12 \\ -\ 9 \\ \hline 3 \end{array}$ | $\begin{array}{r} 15 \\ -\ 7 \\ \hline 8 \end{array}$ | $\begin{array}{r} 11 \\ -\ 4 \\ \hline 7 \end{array}$ | $\begin{array}{r} 10 \\ -\ 7 \\ \hline 3 \end{array}$ | $\begin{array}{r} 11 \\ -\ 7 \\ \hline 4 \end{array}$ |

E.
| $\begin{array}{r} 12 \\ -\ 6 \\ \hline 6 \end{array}$ | $\begin{array}{r} 13 \\ -\ 7 \\ \hline 6 \end{array}$ | $\begin{array}{r} 12 \\ -\ 8 \\ \hline 4 \end{array}$ | $\begin{array}{r} 13 \\ -\ 9 \\ \hline 4 \end{array}$ |

F.
| $\begin{array}{r} 11 \\ -\ 5 \\ \hline 6 \end{array}$ | $\begin{array}{r} 12 \\ -\ 7 \\ \hline 5 \end{array}$ | $\begin{array}{r} 13 \\ -\ 8 \\ \hline 5 \end{array}$ | $\begin{array}{r} 14 \\ -\ 6 \\ \hline 8 \end{array}$ |

Page 73

Subtraction facts to 15

Ace!

Subtract.

A. $11 - 2 = 9$ | $12 - 9 = 3$

B. $11 - 5 = 6$ | $13 - 4 = 9$

C. $12 - 8 = 4$ | $12 - 4 = 8$

D. $11 - 7 = 4$ | $12 - 5 = 7$

E. $13 - 8 = 5$ | $15 - 8 = 7$

F. $14 - 9 = 5$ | $11 - 6 = 5$

G. $11 - 3 = 8$ | $11 - 8 = 3$

H. $14 - 7 = 7$ | $12 - 7 = 5$

I. $13 - 7 = 6$ | $14 - 6 = 8$

J. $15 - 9 = 6$ | $15 - 7 = 8$

K. $13 - 6 = 7$ | $12 - 3 = 9$

Page 74

Subtraction facts to 18

Reach Your Peak

Subtract.

A.
| $\begin{array}{r} 16 \\ -\ 7 \\ \hline 9 \end{array}$ | $\begin{array}{r} 10 \\ -\ 6 \\ \hline 4 \end{array}$ | $\begin{array}{r} 11 \\ -\ 7 \\ \hline 4 \end{array}$ | $\begin{array}{r} 12 \\ -\ 4 \\ \hline 8 \end{array}$ | $\begin{array}{r} 14 \\ -\ 6 \\ \hline 8 \end{array}$ |

B.
| $\begin{array}{r} 11 \\ -\ 2 \\ \hline 9 \end{array}$ | $\begin{array}{r} 13 \\ -\ 7 \\ \hline 6 \end{array}$ | $\begin{array}{r} 16 \\ -\ 6 \\ \hline 10 \end{array}$ | $\begin{array}{r} 11 \\ -\ 5 \\ \hline 6 \end{array}$ | $\begin{array}{r} 12 \\ -\ 7 \\ \hline 5 \end{array}$ |

C.
| $\begin{array}{r} 11 \\ -\ 9 \\ \hline 2 \end{array}$ | $\begin{array}{r} 15 \\ -\ 9 \\ \hline 6 \end{array}$ | $\begin{array}{r} 13 \\ -\ 4 \\ \hline 9 \end{array}$ | $\begin{array}{r} 16 \\ -\ 8 \\ \hline 8 \end{array}$ | $\begin{array}{r} 14 \\ -\ 9 \\ \hline 5 \end{array}$ | $\begin{array}{r} 10 \\ -\ 7 \\ \hline 3 \end{array}$ | $\begin{array}{r} 10 \\ -\ 5 \\ \hline 5 \end{array}$ |

D.
| $\begin{array}{r} 14 \\ -\ 8 \\ \hline 6 \end{array}$ | $\begin{array}{r} 17 \\ -\ 7 \\ \hline 10 \end{array}$ | $\begin{array}{r} 12 \\ -\ 8 \\ \hline 4 \end{array}$ | $\begin{array}{r} 11 \\ -\ 4 \\ \hline 7 \end{array}$ | $\begin{array}{r} 17 \\ -\ 7 \\ \hline 10 \end{array}$ | $\begin{array}{r} 15 \\ -\ 5 \\ \hline 10 \end{array}$ | $\begin{array}{r} 12 \\ -\ 3 \\ \hline 9 \end{array}$ |

E.
| $\begin{array}{r} 14 \\ -\ 5 \\ \hline 9 \end{array}$ | $\begin{array}{r} 18 \\ -\ 9 \\ \hline 9 \end{array}$ | $\begin{array}{r} 14 \\ -\ 4 \\ \hline 10 \end{array}$ | $\begin{array}{r} 13 \\ -\ 9 \\ \hline 4 \end{array}$ | $\begin{array}{r} 11 \\ -\ 8 \\ \hline 3 \end{array}$ | $\begin{array}{r} 12 \\ -\ 6 \\ \hline 6 \end{array}$ | $\begin{array}{r} 13 \\ -\ 5 \\ \hline 8 \end{array}$ |

F. $13 - 8 = 5$ | $17 - 9 = 8$ | $11 - 6 = 5$

G. $12 - 5 = 7$ | $13 - 3 = 10$ | $12 - 9 = 3$

H. $15 - 7 = 8$ | $15 - 6 = 9$ | $14 - 7 = 7$

Page 75

Subtraction facts to 18

Make the Goal

Subtract.

A. $12 - 5 = 7$ | $12 - 3 = 9$ | $11 - 7 = 4$

B. $11 - 8 = 3$ | $14 - 7 = 7$ | $12 - 8 = 4$

C. $11 - 5 = 6$ | $13 - 7 = 6$ | $16 - 9 = 7$

D.
| $\begin{array}{r} 11 \\ -\ 3 \\ \hline 8 \end{array}$ | $\begin{array}{r} 12 \\ -\ 9 \\ \hline 3 \end{array}$ | $\begin{array}{r} 14 \\ -\ 9 \\ \hline 5 \end{array}$ | $\begin{array}{r} 14 \\ -\ 5 \\ \hline 9 \end{array}$ | $\begin{array}{r} 11 \\ -\ 9 \\ \hline 2 \end{array}$ | $\begin{array}{r} 17 \\ -\ 7 \\ \hline 10 \end{array}$ | $\begin{array}{r} 10 \\ -\ 4 \\ \hline 6 \end{array}$ |

E.
| $\begin{array}{r} 15 \\ -\ 9 \\ \hline 6 \end{array}$ | $\begin{array}{r} 13 \\ -\ 5 \\ \hline 8 \end{array}$ | $\begin{array}{r} 12 \\ -\ 4 \\ \hline 8 \end{array}$ | $\begin{array}{r} 14 \\ -\ 8 \\ \hline 6 \end{array}$ | $\begin{array}{r} 16 \\ -\ 7 \\ \hline 9 \end{array}$ | $\begin{array}{r} 12 \\ -\ 6 \\ \hline 6 \end{array}$ | $\begin{array}{r} 14 \\ -\ 4 \\ \hline 10 \end{array}$ |

F.
| $\begin{array}{r} 13 \\ -\ 4 \\ \hline 9 \end{array}$ | $\begin{array}{r} 12 \\ -\ 7 \\ \hline 5 \end{array}$ | $\begin{array}{r} 17 \\ -\ 8 \\ \hline 9 \end{array}$ | $\begin{array}{r} 11 \\ -\ 2 \\ \hline 9 \end{array}$ | $\begin{array}{r} 13 \\ -\ 6 \\ \hline 7 \end{array}$ | $\begin{array}{r} 16 \\ -\ 6 \\ \hline 10 \end{array}$ | $\begin{array}{r} 10 \\ -\ 6 \\ \hline 4 \end{array}$ |

G.
| $\begin{array}{r} 18 \\ -\ 9 \\ \hline 9 \end{array}$ | $\begin{array}{r} 16 \\ -\ 8 \\ \hline 8 \end{array}$ | $\begin{array}{r} 15 \\ -\ 6 \\ \hline 9 \end{array}$ | $\begin{array}{r} 13 \\ -\ 8 \\ \hline 5 \end{array}$ |

H.
| $\begin{array}{r} 17 \\ -\ 9 \\ \hline 8 \end{array}$ | $\begin{array}{r} 15 \\ -\ 7 \\ \hline 8 \end{array}$ | $\begin{array}{r} 15 \\ -\ 8 \\ \hline 7 \end{array}$ | $\begin{array}{r} 13 \\ -\ 9 \\ \hline 4 \end{array}$ |

Page 76

123

FS-32068 First Grade Math Review

Answer Key

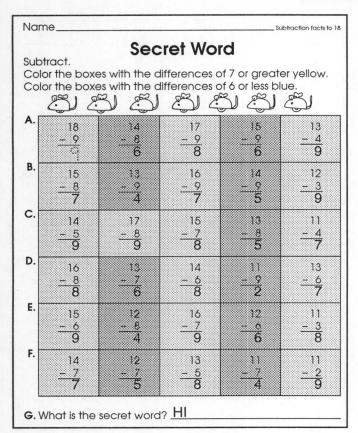

Page 77

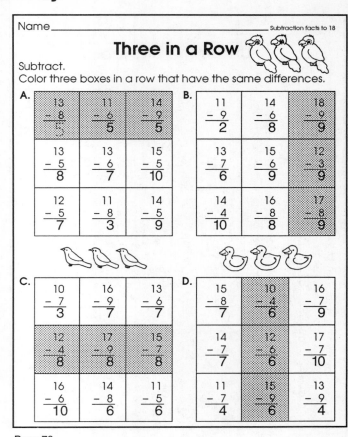

Page 78

Page 79

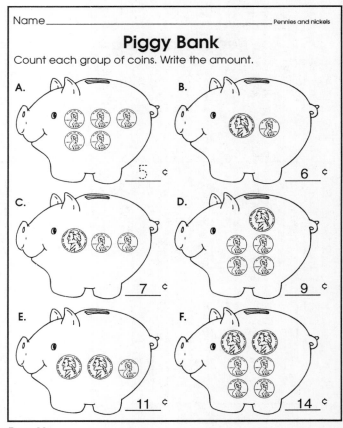

Page 80

FS-32068 First Grade Math Review

Answer Key

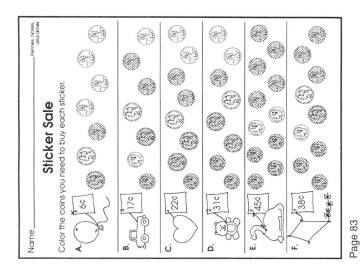

Name _____

Pennies, nickels, and dimes

Sticker Sale

Color the coins you need to buy each sticker.

A. 6¢

B. 17¢

C. 22¢

D. 31¢

E. 45¢

F. 38¢

Page 83

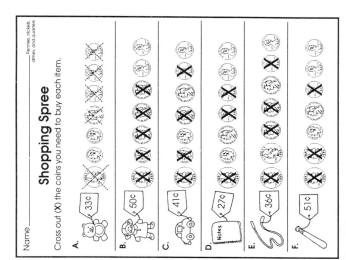

Name _____

Pennies, nickels, dimes, and quarters

Shopping Spree

Cross out (X) the coins you need to buy each item.

A. 33¢

B. 50¢

C. 41¢

D. 27¢

E. 36¢

F. 51¢

Page 86

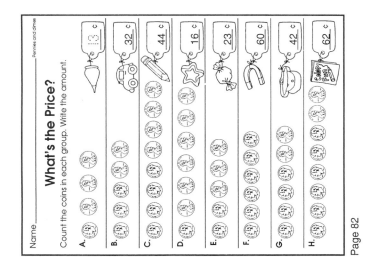

Name _____

Pennies and dimes

What's the Price?

Count the coins in each group. Write the amount.

A. ___ ¢

B. 32 ¢

C. 44 ¢

D. 16 ¢

E. 23 ¢

F. 60 ¢

G. 42 ¢

H. 62 ¢

Page 82

Name _____

Pennies, nickels, dimes, and quarters

Money Match

Match each group of coins to the correct amount.

A. 33¢

B. 38¢

C. 29¢

D. 41¢

E. 51¢

F. 65¢

G. 57¢

H. 75¢

Page 85

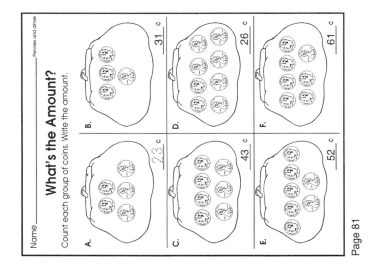

Name _____

Pennies and dimes

What's the Amount?

Count each group of coins. Write the amount.

A. 23 ¢

B. 31 ¢

C. 43 ¢

D. 26 ¢

E. 52 ¢

F. 61 ¢

Page 81

Name _____

Pennies, nickels, and dimes

Change Box

Count each group of coins. Write the amount.

A. 38 ¢

B. 54 ¢

C. 48 ¢

___ ¢

33 ¢

67 ¢

Page 84

FS-32068 First Grade Math Review

Answer Key

Name _____

What Time Is It?

Circle the correct time.

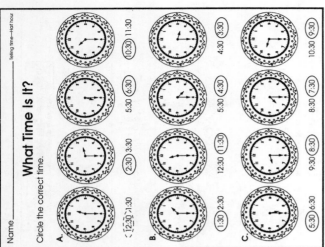

A.
(12:30) 1:30   2:30 3:30   (10:30) 11:30

B.
1:30 2:30   12:30 (11:30)   5:30 (6:30)

C.
(5:30) 6:30   9:30 (8:30)   4:30 (3:30)

5:30 (4:30)   8:30 (7:30)   10:30 (9:30)

Page 89

Telling Time—Hour

Name _____

Show the Time

Draw the hands on each clock to show the time.

A. 5:00   3:00   7:00

B. 9:00   1:00   6:00

C. 4:00   2:00   12:00

Page 88

Telling Time—Hour

Name _____

Telling Time

Write the time.

A. 1:00   2:00   3:00

B. 9:00   10:00   11:00

C. 4:00   8:00   12:00

Page 87

Calendar

Name _____

The Calendar

This month has 31 days.
It begins on Monday.
Write the days.

May

Sunday	Monday	Tuesday	Wednesday	Thursday	Friday	Saturday
	----	2	3	4	5	6
7	8	9	10	11	12	13
14	15	16	17	18	19	20
21	22	23	24	25	26	27
28	29	30	31			

Answer the questions.

A. What date is the third Wednesday in May? __May 17__

B. How many Sundays are in this month? __four__

C. What date is between May 8 and May 10? __May 9__

D. What day of the week is the fifth? __Friday__

E. Starting on the 19th, how many days until the end of the month? __12 days__

Page 92

Calendar

Name _____

It's a Date!

This month has 30 days.
It begins on Wednesday.
Write the dates.

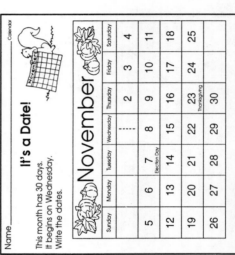

November

Sunday	Monday	Tuesday	Wednesday	Thursday	Friday	Saturday
			----	2	3	4
5	6	7 Election Day	8	9	10	11
12	13	14	15	16	17	18
19	20	21	22	23 Thanksgiving	24	25
26	27	28	29	30		

Answer the questions.

A. What date is Election Day? __November 7__

B. How many Wednesdays are in November? __five__

C. What date is Thanksgiving? __November 23__

D. How many Sundays are there in this month? __four__

E. What day of the week is November 13? __Monday__

F. What day of the week is November 30? __Thursday__

Page 91

Telling time—Half hour

Name _____

What's the Time?

Draw a line from each clock to the matching time.

A. 7:30   10:30   3:30   12:30

B. 1:30   2:30   8:30   6:30

C. 9:30   4:30   11:30   5:30

Page 90

© Frank Schaffer Publications, Inc.

126

FS-32068 First Grade Math Review

Answer Key

Name _____

Coloring Fractions

The parts that are colored may vary.

Possible answers.

A. Color $\frac{1}{2}$.

B. Color $\frac{1}{3}$.

C. Color $\frac{1}{4}$.

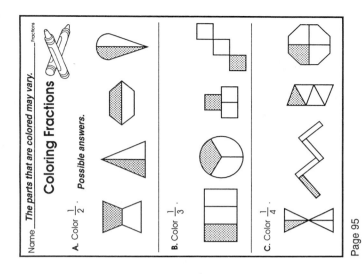

Page 95

Name _____

Fraction Match

Draw lines to match.

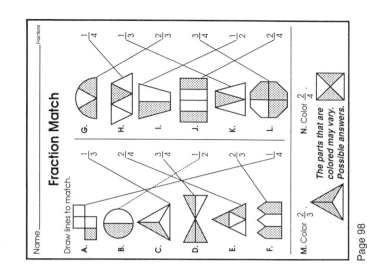

M. Color $\frac{2}{3}$.

N. Color $\frac{2}{4}$.

The parts that are colored may vary. Possible answers.

Page 98

Name _____

Equal Parts Fun

A. Color the shapes that have two equal parts.

B. Color the shapes that have three equal parts.

C. Color the shapes that have four equal parts.

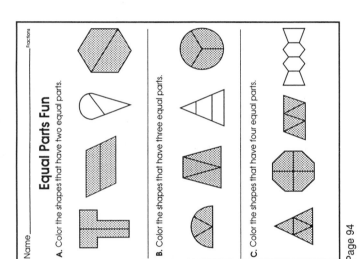

Page 94

Name _____

Colored arrangements of the parts may vary.

Fractions

Possible answers.

A. Color $\frac{1}{2}$ blue.
Color $\frac{1}{2}$ red.

B. Color $\frac{1}{3}$ green.
Color $\frac{1}{3}$ yellow.
Color $\frac{1}{3}$ orange.

C. Color $\frac{1}{4}$ purple.
Color $\frac{1}{4}$ red.
Color $\frac{2}{4}$ green.

D. Color $\frac{2}{3}$ blue.
Color $\frac{1}{3}$ green.

E. Color $\frac{1}{4}$ yellow.
Color $\frac{3}{4}$ red.

F. Color $\frac{3}{4}$ blue.
Color $\frac{1}{4}$ orange.

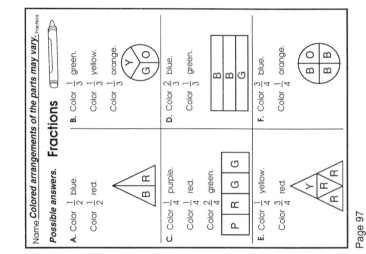

Page 97

Name _____

Equal Parts

Write the number of equal parts.

A. __2__ equal parts

B. __4__ equal parts

C. __3__ equal parts

D. __2__ equal parts

E. __3__ equal parts

F. __2__ equal parts

G. __3__ equal parts

H. __4__ equal parts

Page 93

Name _____

The parts that are colored may vary.

Finding Fractions

Possible answers.

A. Color $\frac{1}{2}$ if it has equal parts.

B. Color $\frac{1}{3}$ if it has equal parts.

C. Color $\frac{1}{4}$ if it has equal parts.

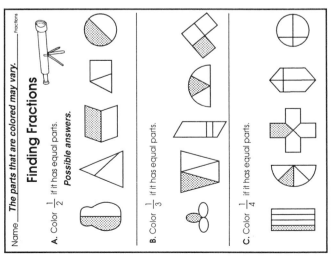

Page 96

Answer Key

Sailing Through Subtraction
Two-digit subtraction—No regrouping

Name _____

Subtract.

A. 47 − 23 = 24 | 56 − 23 = 33 | 67 − 36 = 31 | 39 − 14 = 25
B. 59 − 41 = 18 | 48 − 15 = 33 | 25 − 20 = 05 | 64 − 51 = 13
C. 83 − 73 = 10 | 95 − 62 = 33 | 76 − 53 = 23 | 32 − 11 = 21
D. 98 − 34 = 64 | 87 − 26 = 61 | 49 − 35 = 14

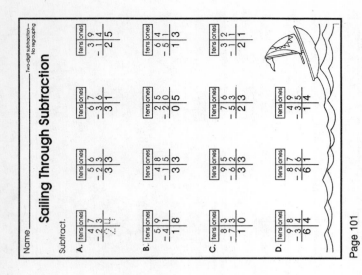

Page 101

Champions
Two-digit addition and subtraction—No regrouping

Name _____

Add.

A. 32 + 56 = 88 | 86 + 12 = 98 | 83 + 14 = 97 | 42 + 15 = 57 | 64 + 21 = 85 | 26 + 33 = 59 | 13 + 66 = 79
B. 36 + 52 = 88 | 54 + 23 = 77 | 41 + 53 = 94 | 72 + 20 = 92 | 37 + 51 = 88 | 15 + 32 = 47 | 80 + 16 = 96
C. 19 + 30 = 49 | 76 + 22 = 98 | 54 + 34 = 88 | 62 + 25 = 87 | 18 + 71 = 89 | 24 + 32 = 56 | 13 + 36 = 49

Subtract.

D. 98 − 43 = 55 | 79 − 25 = 54 | 57 − 21 = 36 | 39 − 13 = 26 | 89 − 29 = 60 | 85 − 41 = 44 | 35 − 24 = 11
E. 49 − 32 = 17 | 59 − 41 = 18 | 73 − 21 = 52 | 66 − 23 = 43
F. 83 − 51 = 32 | 27 − 15 = 12 | 39 − 18 = 21 | 46 − 32 = 14

Page 104

A Garden of Problems
Two-digit addition—No regrouping

Name _____

Add.

A. 25 + ? = 33 | 42 + 23 = 65 | 47 + 31 = 78 | 36 + 43 = 79
B. 35 + 24 = 59 | 52 + 42 = 94 | 32 + 26 = 58 | 26 + 53 = 79
C. 15 + 70 = 85 | 27 + 42 = 69 | 44 + 55 = 99 | 74 + 12 = 86
D. 51 + 10 = 61 | 70 + 21 = 91 | 65 + 23 = 88 | 81 + 18 = 99

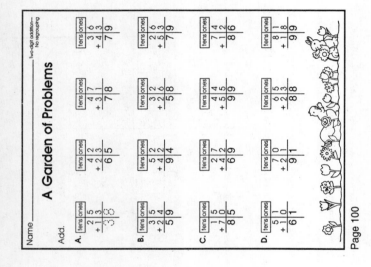

Page 100

What a Ride!
Two-digit addition and subtraction—No regrouping

Name _____

Add.

A. 23 + 16 = 39 | 59 + 20 = 79 | 21 + 37 = 58 | 51 + 26 = 77 | 14 + 63 = 77 | 80 + 19 = 99
B. 15 + 24 = 39 | 53 + 23 = 76 | 24 + 60 = 84 | 33 + 41 = 74 | 12 + 45 = 57 | 62 + 21 = 83
C. 21 + 27 = 48 | 33 + 52 = 85 | 61 + 23 = 84 | 85 + 12 = 97 | 72 + 17 = 89 | 18 + 71 = 89

Subtract.

D. 48 − 21 = 27 | 83 − 31 = 52 | 78 − 16 = 62 | 49 − 18 = 31 | 68 − 21 = 47 | 78 − 44 = 34
E. 79 − 26 = 53 | 73 − 22 = 51 | 97 − 34 = 63 | 78 − 62 = 16 | 57 − 12 = 45 | 68 − 36 = 32 | 94 − 52 = 42

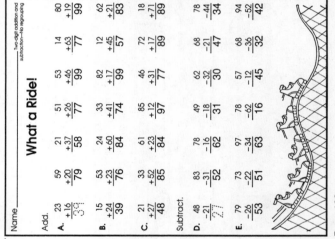

Page 103

Dinosaur Sums
Two-digit addition—No regrouping

Name _____

Add.

A. 23 + 14 = 37 | 25 + 22 = 47 | 18 + 21 = 39 | 15 + 63 = 78
B. 53 + 15 = 68 | 38 + 31 = 69 | 40 + 27 = 67 | 19 + 70 = 89
C. 81 + 12 = 93 | 37 + 22 = 59 | 26 + 52 = 78 | 10 + 70 = 80
D. 63 + 36 = 99 | 43 + 56 = 99 | 24 + 35 = 59 | 60 + 23 = 83

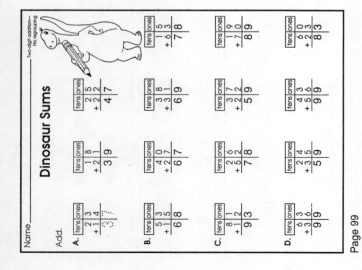

Page 99

Bear Problems
Two-digit subtraction—No regrouping

Name _____

Subtract.

A. 35 − 13 = 22 | 56 − 15 = 41 | 47 − 36 = 11 | 95 − 34 = 61
B. 23 − 13 = 10 | 81 − 70 = 11 | 75 − 42 = 33 | 45 − 20 = 25
C. 86 − 43 = 43 | 58 − 48 = 10 | 79 − 68 = 11 | 99 − 53 = 46
D. 33 − 13 = 21 | 17 − 10 = 07 | 28 − 14 = 14

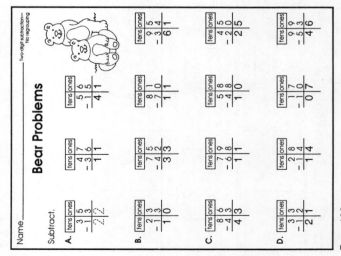

Page 102

FS-32068 First Grade Math Review